WHERE SOUL & SPIRIT MEET

Praying with the Bible

MARILYN MORGAN HELLEBERG

Abingdon Press / Nashville

WHERE SOUL AND SPIRIT MEET

Copyright © 1986 by Abingdon Press

This book is printed on acid-free paper.

Library of Congress Cataloging-in-Publication Data

HELLEBERG, MARILYN M.
  Where soul and spirit meet.
  1. Bible—Reading. 2. Prayer. 3. Bible—Meditations.
  4. Spiritual exercises. I. Title.
  BS617.H45   1986   242'.5   86-1020

ISBN 0-687-45159-0 (pbk.: alk. paper)

Grateful acknowledgement is made for the following:
From Servant Books, permission to quote from *Reading Scripture as the Word of God,* © 1975 by George Martin.
From the Paulist Press, permission to adapt material from *Beyond TM: A Practical Guide to the Lost Traditions of Christian Meditation,* © 1980 by Marilyn Morgan Helleberg.
Adaptation of "How to: Be a Daily Prayer", Marilyn Morgan Helleberg. Reprinted with permission from Guideposts Magazine. Copyright © 1982 by Guideposts Associates, Inc., Carmel, New York 10512.
Excerpt reprinted with permission from *DAILY GUIDEPOSTS, 1982* (Oct. 18, pp. 301-311; Oct. 20, p. 56) Marilyn Morgan Helleberg. Copyright © 1982 by Guideposts Associates, Inc., Carmel, New York 10512.
Excerpt reprinted with permission from *DAILY GUIDEPOSTS, 1980* (Jan. 17, p. 15; May 17, p. 125) Marilyn Morgan Helleberg. Copyright © 1980 by Guideposts Associates, Inc., Carmel, New York 10512.
Excerpt reprinted with permission from *DAILY GUIDEPOSTS, 1979* (Oct. 30, pp. 259-260) Marilyn Morgan Helleberg. Copyright © 1978 by Guideposts Associates, Inc., Carmel, New York 10512.
Adapted from "Who's Boss Around Here?" by Bill Burke (Marilyn Morgan Helleberg). Reprinted by permission from Guideposts Magazine. Copyright © 1979 by Guideposts Associates, Inc., Carmel, New York 10512.

MANUFACTURED BY THE PARTHENON PRESS AT
NASHVILLE, TENNESSEE, UNITED STATES OF AMERICA

Composition by Compositor's, Cedar Rapids, Iowa.

To my mother,
Helen Banta Morgan.
"May light perpetual
shine upon her."

CONTENTS

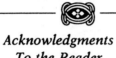

Acknowledgments **7**
To the Reader **9**

Part I—Scriptural Prayer **11**
How Does Praying with Your Bible Differ
from Studying It? **19**
What Happens in Scriptural Prayer? **20**
Notes **24**

Part II—The Procedure **25**
Before Starting **28**
Bible Study Time **30**
The Prayer Time **32**
Preventive Maintenance **37**
Summary **40**
Notes **41**

Part III—Themes and Scriptures **43**
Week 1 • "I invite you" **45**
Week 2 • "I want to speak to you
through My Word" **47**
Week 3 • "I love you with a creating love" **48**
Week 4 • "I love you with a providing
and caring love" **50**
Week 5 • "Do not be discouraged" **52**
Week 6 • "I love you, anyway" **53**

Week 7 • "I want you to be happy"   **55**

Week 8 • "Do not be afraid.
I will protect you"   **57**

Week 9 • "When you have too much to do,
I will help you accomplish it"   **58**

Week 10 • "I will guide your decisions"   **60**

Week 11 • "Prepare ye the way"   **62**

Week 12 • "I give you My Son"   **63**

Week 13 • "I was human like you"   **66**

Week 14 • "Follow Me"   **67**

Week 15 • "I will teach you"   **69**

Week 16 • "I will heal the sick"   **72**

Week 17 • "This is the way to love"   **74**

Week 18 • "I am"   **76**

Week 19 • "I offer you gentleness,
compassion, forgiveness"   **79**

Week 20 • "I will help you fight temptation"   **81**

Week 21 • "I will set you free"   **83**

Week 22 • "I will help you overcome your anger"
86

Week 23 • "I invite you to share in My last meal
with My disciples"   **89**

Week 24 • "I give you My life"   **90**

Week 25 • "I have conquered death.
Come live with Me"   **92**

Week 26 • "I am with you always.
Look for Me in all things"   **94**

Week 27 • "I will give you peace"   **96**

Week 28 • "I am here to comfort you"   **97**

Week 29 • "I will pray in you"   **99**

Week 30 • "I am the Living Water"   **101**

Part IV—Where Do We Go from Here?   **105**

Appendix   **109**

ACKNOWLEDGMENTS

THIS book did not come about by my efforts alone. All through the writing of it, I have been conscious of the movement of the Holy Spirit, guiding my thoughts, supplying me with words, and directing me to appropriate Scriptures. I mention this because I want you to know that whatever there is of value in it comes from Him and not from me.

I have also had some very fine human help. I wish to express my deepest gratitude and indebtedness to Father Joseph B. Smerke, O.S.C., of the Crosier Renewal Center in Hastings, Nebraska. It was through his excellent spiritual direction and guidance that I first learned to pray with Scripture. I attended a Scriptural Prayer Retreat given by Father Smerke several years ago, and I have incorporated many of his ideas into this book.

Special thanks to my good friend, Dorothy Olson, whose knowledge of the Bible prompted me to ask her to read the manuscript. The changes she suggested have enhanced the work.

I also wish to express my appreciation to *Guideposts* for

giving me permission to retell, in these pages, some of my personal experiences that originally appeared in the *Daily Guideposts* devotional volumes.

Thanks, also, to Avery Brooke, whose interest in my work has encouraged me along the way and whose own books indicate that we are spiritual sisters.

Finally, I'd like to thank all of those who have attended my retreats and whose stories have provided real-life examples of the ways in which God changes lives through praying with your Bible. Because prayer is a very personal interchange between an individual and God, I have not used the real names of those whose experiences I've described in these pages. To further preserve their anonymity, I have also changed some of the circumstances.

TO THE READER

This book was written for those who want to develop a deeper, more intimate relationship with our Lord. This takes time. I don't mean to imply that the book is difficult to read. It isn't. I have written in a simple, conversational style, just as I would converse with you over a cup of coffee, but the content must be sipped and savored, rather than gulped.

Parts I and II may be read in one sitting, but the Themes and Scriptures of Part III are designed to be used over a thirty-week period of deepening levels of spiritual awareness. So please, do not read through the themes one after another, but take them separately, a week at a time.

Although your prayer time itself will be private and personal, this material lends itself beautifully to follow-up by Bible study groups, prayer groups, and adult church school classes. At the beginning of each group session, time should be allowed for sharing and discussion of what the Lord has said to each person through the assigned Scriptures. Members should never be made to feel any pressure to talk about their experiences of prayer, but the opportunity should be given. Using the thirty-week plan as a group will help everyone to stay faithful to their commitment to pray daily.

Members of such groups soon become aware of a certain quiet bonding that takes place among them as they share the ways in which God is speaking to them through His Word.

PART I

Scriptural Prayer

*And they said one to another, Did not our heart
burn within us, while he talked with us by the way,
and while he opened to us the Scriptures?*

Luke 24:32

I**T** was early December when the phone call came from
Omaha. "This is Carol Chapman. Do you remember
me?"

Of course I remembered! I'd never met her, but she had
called me a few weeks before, after reading my book on
Christian meditation. She had asked for my prayers for
her nephew, Steven Fuesz, and I'd been praying for him
every day since her call. Steven was thirteen and the
victim of a rare form of acute leukemia. Somehow, during the weeks I'd been praying for him, he'd become
wrapped within the mothering part of my heart, even
though we'd never met. Maybe it was because Steven was
the same age as my own son, John. Maybe it was because
I was so moved by his unshakeable faith. He told his
family doctor and his oncologist that God was going to
heal him, and he prayed for all the other children in the
hospital.

"They've told Linda and Bill to take Steven home from the hospital and have Christmas early," Carol continued, "because he probably won't live till December twenty-fifth. They really need your prayers, Marilyn!"

I stared, unseeing, at the poinsettia pictured on the desk calendar. How was I to pray, under the shadow of this black news? Since I'd been leading prayer retreats and writing for Christian publications, I'd often prayed with and for people for healing. But this was different. A child was dying.

As soon as we finished talking I went to my "prayer chair" in the living room, and as I reached for my Bible, I prayed, "Lord, please give me something for Steven." Then I opened to the place where my marker was. I'd been reading a little bit each day from the Gospel of Mark, and I was halfway through chapter 5. I began reading:

> "And a certain woman, which had an issue of blood twelve years, And had suffered many things of many physicians, and had spent all that she had, and was nothing bettered, but rather grew worse, When she had heard of Jesus, came in the press behind, and touched his garment. For she said, If I may touch but his clothes, I shall be whole. And straightway the fountain of her blood was dried up; and she felt in her body that she was healed of that plague. And Jesus, immediately knowing in himself that virtue had gone out of him, turned him about in the press, and said, Who touched my clothes? And his disciples said unto him, Thou seest the multitude thronging thee, and sayest thou, Who touched me? And he looked round about to see her that had done this thing. But the woman fearing and trembling, knowing what was done in her, came and fell down before him, and

told him all the truth. And he said unto her, Daughter, thy faith hath made thee whole; go in peace, and be whole of thy plague."

(Mark 5:25–34)

My heart was brimming with thanksgiving as I closed my Bible. Time after time, since I've been praying with Scripture, God has spoken to me so specifically through His Word that I've become stunned with a sharp awareness of His living presence with me at that moment.

I closed my eyes and imagined myself standing with young Steven on that dusty road as Jesus and His disciples came walking toward us. They were surrounded by great multitudes of people, all clamoring for the Master's attention. In my mind's eye, I took Steven's hand and reached past all those people until his fingers touched the shining white robe of Jesus. At that instant, a brilliant light seemed to enter into Steven's body . . . I looked at my watch. It was 9:00 A.M. I spent the rest of my prayer time in praise and thanksgiving and then wrote a letter to Steven, telling him about my prayer.

A few days later, I received a letter from Steven's mother. After three days of praying for faith, Steven had awakened Saturday morning, climbed the stairs to his parents' room, and announced, "Now I finally have enough faith to pray for complete healing."

The time? 9:00 A.M.—the exact time that God gave me the prayer for Steven, from the fifth chapter of Mark.

Steven's color and strength began to come back and the sores on his body started to heal. When they took him back for testing ten days later, the blood that was supposedly so diseased had miraculously returned to normal levels (white blood count, hemoglobin, hematocrit, the differential and the platelet count)!

Steven and his family had the happiest Christmas of

their lives and they didn't have to have it early. And when school started, this child who had been sent home to die rejoined his classmates.

I wish this were the end of the story, but it isn't.

It was July when Carol called to say that Steven had suffered a serious relapse. Her words throbbed against my heart: ". . . hospital in Illinois . . . 105 degree fever . . . blood count dangerously low . . . constant pain . . . doctors given up. . . ." Again they asked for my prayers and again I felt so desperately inadequate. But the Lord was not depending on my adequacy! This time, He gave me the 91st Psalm for Steven, so I wrote and asked if someone would read it to him. His mother called a few days later to say, "Steven keeps asking us to read it over and over again. It has become his lifeline."

An August phone call said Steven was again being sent home to die. Could they stop at my house for prayer, on their way back to Colorado?

"Of course!" As soon as I hung up the phone, I read the Bible verses for the day. Again, I was stunned by the appropriateness of the verses. The one that seemed most poignant was Matthew 10:39: "He that loseth his life for my sake shall find it."

The Fueszes arrived at my house in the early afternoon. As I put my arms around Steven's frail, feverish body, love and pain stabbed at my heart. We affirmed that the love of Jesus was surrounding, enfolding, and entering into Steven's body, soul, and spirit. Then that child, matured by suffering and grace, offered his life to Jesus, "to use me in whatever way You want to use me." By the time they left, Steven's temperature was normal and his pain was gone. He continued to get better after returning home and even started to school in late August.

Then one September night when I returned home from a meeting, there was a message that the Fueszes had called. Steven had almost died the night before, and now he wanted me to pray with him on the phone. Again, that stabbing feeling in my heart. Now I understood why people often avoid the dying and their families. What could I possibly say to Steven? How could I pray for him? I felt so clumsy, so unfit for the task I'd been given. "Oh Lord Jesus, help me, please! Give me the right words!"

Once again I reached for my Bible. The passage for the day was Hebrews 6:1–10, but I got only as far as the first verse when our Lord stopped me. The words were ". . . let us go on unto perfection. . . ." I was blank. "How am I to use those words, Lord?" Silence. Nothing. It was getting late. Fearful and unsure of myself, I breathed a prayer, sat down at the kitchen counter, and dialed Steven's number. As soon as I heard the pain in that young voice I'd learned to love, I knew why our Lord had given me those words from Hebrews.

I opened my mouth and the words that came out seemed to come from beyond me. "Jesus said the kingdom of God is within you, Steven. If you could peel away all the layers of skin and flesh and bones and organs that make up your body, there would still be a self that you would recognize as your own unique spirit. This part of you is untouched by sickness, or pain, or fear. It is perfect." Then we asked the Lord to help Steven get in touch with that perfectly well part of himself—his God-given, immortal spirit. As we prayed, I heard Steven sigh. It was the kind of sigh a baby makes as it nestles into its mother's arms after crying.

At the end of our prayer, Steven said, "I have a temperature of 103, I've been vomiting all day, I'm almost blind, and I'm in terrible pain." Then, in a calmly triumphant voice, wise beyond his years, Steven said, "But my spirit doesn't have leukemia! And in my heart, there's a beautiful, divine peace."

It was the last time we talked. Steven died on September 22. His last words were, "Don't be afraid, Mom and Dad. I'm going to be all right."

There's an ache in me tonight, as I sit in my little basement office sharing Steven's story with you. The loss is so new, and there are still things I want to say to him. Things like . . .

Steven dear, your whole life was a miracle. Your beautiful faith, the peace you found, the way you died—all miracles. And now at last, you've found that perfect wholeness we prayed for. You were right, my young friend. You will be all right. I'm sure of it. Your spirit doesn't have leukemia!

As I look back on Steven's illness and our prayers for him, there are still unanswered questions in my mind. I don't know why he was allowed that period of perfect health. I don't know why the disease returned, or why Steven died. But one thing I do know for sure. God was in control, every minute. I know this not only because of Steven's words but also because of the solid, positive way the Lord guided our prayers, through the channel of Scripture. This was not at all a matter of the "lucky dip," in which you ask a question and open the Bible to any page, hoping for an answer. That may be effective sometimes, but I certainly wouldn't count on it. On the contrary, God guided our prayers for Steven as the result of a very specific way of praying. It's a very exciting form of prayer—one that you'll be discovering in the following pages.

During the past few years, since I've been praying with the Bible, my Friend Jesus has been stepping out of the pages of my Bible in new and glorious ways. For the first time in my life, I feel I know Jesus. Scriptural prayer has been, for me, a life-transfiguring experience.

HOW DOES PRAYING WITH YOUR BIBLE DIFFER FROM STUDYING IT?

"For the word of God is living and active," says Hebrews 4:12 (NASB). That's absolutely true, but the way that livingness takes root in my heart and grows there is a two-part process. I need to approach the Word, first as a reader and then as a listener. Either activity, by itself, is incomplete and lacking in the fullness of His presence.

For me, the only valid reason for reading and studying the Bible is to come into a closer relationship with God Himself, Whose living presence communicates itself to me through the words of Scripture. I want to learn about Him, but even more, I want to come to know Him. To know and not to have that knowledge come alive would be sterile. What I come to know by reading and studying His Word needs to be interiorized, personalized, so that I may come into direct contact with the One Who speaks. I want to know what He said, but I also want to hear Him saying it to me now.

I love home-baked bread, don't you? Even though bread from the grocery store may feed my body adequately, there's something about the aroma, the texture, the taste of the home-baked kind that nourishes my soul as well as my body. And yet, to get that extra special dimension, I have to do some work. The ingredients have to be rounded up, mixed, and kneaded. The dough has to rise, be kneaded again, rise again, be shaped, brushed with butter, and baked. But it's not until the bread is eaten, savored, and digested that the body is nourished.

Just as assembling ingredients, mixing, and kneading are essential steps in making bread, so Bible reading and Bible study are essential steps in learning to hear God speak through His Word. If I skip this important process, I may end up getting a garbled message from my listening. I need to keep growing in my familiarity with the Bible and my ability to find my way through it. I need to understand the context in which a particular passage appears, its historical perspective, something about the person who recorded the words, and how this book, chapter, and verse intertwine with other parts of the Bible.

Then, after studying a passage, I need to set it aside for a while so that, like the rising of the bread, the Word can grow within me.

Finally, the happy culmination toward which all of these efforts have been aimed can occur. The bread may be eaten. "Thy words were found . . . and thy word was unto me the joy and rejoicing of mine heart" (Jeremiah 15:16). Now at last, I can actually hear God speaking to me, personally, at this moment in His eternity. The Bread of Life rises above its container. The Holy Presence steps out of the pages of my Bible and nestles in my heart. This is Scriptural prayer.

Because there are many excellent sources of materials for Bible *study*, the main focus of this book will be on the second part of the two-part process described above—feeding on the Word by praying with Scripture.

WHAT HAPPENS IN SCRIPTURAL PRAYER?

You'll understand Scriptural prayer better when you read the next chapter, which describes the procedure, but here are some thoughts to give you an overview.

When I pray with my Bible I allow my inner mind, where soul and spirit meet, to be touched by the Word, and it is truly a transforming experience.

Studies in speech communication have shown that, when two people converse, only a small part of the overall message is communicated in the words themselves. There is a whole field of nonverbal interaction going on, which says much more than the words that are spoken. When we "read the Bible," the printed words are only an outward symbol. When we pray the Scriptures, the very real presence of the Lord speaks personally to us, in a spiritual interaction wholly beyond the limits of words. For this reason, we can read the same text on different days and the Lord will say something different to us each time, depending on our life situation and special needs at the moment, and on His own choice of what He wishes to communicate to us at that time.

Not only do I hear my Lord speaking directly to me in Scriptural prayer, but His Words actually take up residence within me (see John 15:7). As the authors of *Pray Today's Gospel* explain: "The response is not so much in words as in the inner movements of the heart. The words are but the signs of the deeper reality."[1]

When I yield my heart to God the Father as I listen to Him speak, He re-forms me, re-creates me with the help of Jesus, to be closer to His image. It was Jesus who said, "I have called you friends" (John 15:15), and He becomes my intimate Companion; the Holy Spirit becomes God dwelling in me (John 14:16, 20, 23; 1 John 4:13), and the God-breathed Word comes alive in me.

As the Bible becomes God's Word spoken to me, personally at each turn of my life, that Word begins to shape my concerns and my ideas. I begin to experience the living Word of Jesus as I do my family home—a familiar place of security that I can return to each day, knowing I am loved unconditionally; a place that provides me with roots in an uprooting world; a place where I can receive guidance for the specific needs of the moment, a place I can go for rest and shelter and nourishment. "If you make my word your home you will indeed be my disciples" (John 8:31 JB).

George Martin, in his book *Reading Scripture as the*

Word of God, beautifully expresses what happens in Scriptural prayer.

> God will speak to those who prayerfully read the Bible as his Word. He will not speak in an audible voice; he will not even form words in our mind. His speaking will use no other words than the words that we read—but those words will take on meaning and become alive as if God were present speaking them directly to us. We will have a strong sense that the words of scripture are indeed addressed to us and are talking about us; we will have a sense that they have a meaning and application in our own lives and specific situations. The Bible will be not merely God's Word, but God's Word to me.[2]

Speaking of his own experience, Martin writes:

> I had begun reading scripture because I knew it was a good thing to do; now I read eagerly, with a hunger and thirst for the Word of God. I had begun reading scripture because it contained the Word of God; now I experienced that it contained words of God addressed directly to me, speaking to my daily experience of following Christ.[3]

So we need both Bible study and Scriptural prayer in order to fully experience the love of God through His holy Word. And the glory of it is that eventually, by His grace, the knowing and the loving become one.

I like what Evelyn Christenson says about the benefits of spending time in God's Word:

> "My spiritual barometer for years has been 1 John 1:14: 'These things [are written] that your joy may

be full.' I can always measure the amount of time I'm spending in the scriptures by how much joy (not superficial happiness, but deep down abiding joy) I have. When I find a lack of joy in my life, the first thing I check is how much time I'm spending in God's Word!"[4]

In addition to these testimonies, I'd like to close this chapter by quoting a paragraph from my own spiritual journal, written just a week and a half after I started praying the Scriptures.

Oh, what a deeply personal relationship with Christ this is bringing me. I feel that, in each day's Scripture, He has planted something just for me, and I look forward, so eagerly, to the next day's meeting with Him, to see what He'll have to say to me. Several times today, I thought of my newly refound Friend and relished the private trysts my prayer times have become.

My take-away verse today is: "Take my yoke upon you, and learn of me." Jesus seems to be saying to me, "Join yourself to me, and the Father will reveal me to you and I will reveal Him to you." Thank You, Lord. Already that is happening. How real is Your voice. How dear is Your presence.

It is my prayer that you will also experience this kind of deep joy as you pray with your Bible.

NOTES

1. Mischke and Mischke, *Pray Today's Gospel* (New York, N.Y.: Alba House, 1980), p. v.

2. George Martin, *Reading Scripture as the Word of God* (Ann Arbor, Mich.: Servant Books, 1975), p. 61.

3. Ibid., p. 68.

4. Evelyn Christenson, *Lord, Change Me!* (Wheaton, Ill.: Victor Books, 1977), p. 32.

PART II

The Procedure

But he answered and said, It is written, Man shall not live by bread alone, but by every word that proceedeth out of the mouth of God.

Matthew 4:4

WHEN I was a child, my mother hired a delightful German lady to help with the housecleaning once a week. Mrs. Fahrenbrucke, who also worked for several other families, had a husband and eight children of her own. Yet, as busy as she was, her own house was always immaculate. I remember hearing my mother ask her once, "Frieda, how in the world do you do it?" Mrs. Fahrenbrucke smiled and said, in her lovely, rich accent, "Well, it takes a wee bit pattern."

Isn't that true of most things that we value enough to invest part of ourselves in? The suggestions I'm about to give for praying the Scriptures are not pat little formulas for holiness. They are just a "wee bit pattern" to help you get started in praying with your Bible. Once you understand the important points of the procedure and have experienced communion with God by hearing Him speak to you in Scriptural prayer, you won't need the "pattern" anymore. With the help of the Holy Spirit, you will develop your own way of getting in touch with the One Who speaks to you through the Bible.

Don't be overwhelmed by the directions that follow. Praying with Scripture is really quite simple. Just read through the procedural suggestions to get the general idea, and then at the end of the chapter, I'll give a brief summary that will bring it all together in its true simplicity.

BEFORE STARTING

1. *Make a prayer covenant.* In order to really experience the joys of Scriptural prayer, you *must* make a commitment to the Lord to be present with Him in His Word every single day, without fail. Schedule it into your daily routine in the same way you would a lesson or other appointment. On the first day, sit down with your Friend, Jesus, and *write out* your prayer covenant. Then seal it with prayer, acknowledging your own inability to be faithful to it without His help. Then ask for that help.[1]

Plan to spend at least twenty to thirty minutes with God in His Word each day. An hour is not too long. If you think you don't have time to schedule in prayer, I'd suggest you make a list of all the daily demands on your time. Then imagine you're a hundred years old and looking back on your life. From *that* perspective, which things are most important? Which have lasting value?

Don't plan your prayer time when you're likely to be tired or just after a meal. Give God some of your *best* time—the time when you're most alert.

I like the metaphor George Martin uses to emphasize the importance of the daily Bible time.

Reading Scripture is not like taking one's wife out to dinner on special occasions; it must be like the evening supper that husband and wife share, day in, day out. Periodic times of intensive reading of the Bible are a good idea, just as occasional evenings out together build a marriage. But just as our daily supper nourishes us, our daily reading of Scripture will bring the strength of God into our everyday lives. Anything less than daily reading is likely to lead to spiritual malnutrition.[2]

2. *Establish a regular place for prayer.* Having a particular place to pray helps you to settle in more easily, by creating a mental set and an air of expectancy, so that when you enter that special room and sit in that same chair, your mind automatically begins to calm down and tune in to the Lord. It should be a place where you can be alone, without being interrupted. I know this is difficult for many people, but if you really want to do it, you'll find a way. I have a friend who lives in a small apartment with her husband and two little children. She prays in her parked car. It is said that the mother of John and Charles Wesley, who couldn't find a corner in her house to be alone, would sit in a kitchen chair and put her large apron over her head, which said to her family: "Please do not disturb. I am at prayer." I'm sure this was a more eloquent statement to her children about the importance of God in daily life than all the preaching in the world!

3. *Minimize distractions.* Take the phone off the hook, or if someone else is home, ask them to take calls for you to return. If you're home alone, put a note on the outside door. It can be very simple: "Please do not disturb between 11:00 and 11:30 A.M. Thank you." If you can't find a quiet place to pray, buy a pair of earplugs. Because I often have to compete with the TV in the next room, or kids scuffling, or dogs barking, my earplugs have been a

real blessing to me. Until your family gets used to your scheduled prayer time, you may need to post a note on the door of the room where you pray. (Draw a smiley face in the corner to keep the message positive!)

    4. *Assemble materials.*

        a. I'd suggest having at least two versions of the Bible handy. Sometimes the Lord speaks to me through one translation and sometimes through another. There is value in consistently reading one translation so that the phrasing becomes familiar. Then, reading the same passage in a different version will bring out different nuances in familiar passages and provide fresh insights.

        b. For me, the single most valuable item besides my Bibles is my notebook. Any type will do—a spiral, loose leaf, or tablet. It should be fairly sturdy, though, because you'll want to keep it and refer back to it frequently.

        c. Consult Bible study aids. I'll leave this to your discretion. A Bible dictionary, a commentary, and a concordance will be most helpful.

    5. *Locate the passage for the day.* Suggested readings will follow in the remainder of this book. Mark the beginning and ending of the Scripture reading. If you're not in the habit of marking in your Bible, this may bother you at first, but really, there's nothing irreverent about it. The Word of God is meant for personal use, and it will become more and more meaningful as you mark words or phrases that are special to you.

BIBLE STUDY TIME

Now you are ready for the reading and studying part that I compared with the preparation of the ingredients in the bread-making analogy earlier.

So much depends, at this point, on the attitude with which you approach the Bible. There are many levels of meaning to each passage in the Bible. As you study it, these levels keep unfolding. Some are primarily historical, some beautiful, some interesting. But in Scriptural prayer it's important to keep focused on the fact that we are listening for *God's* message and that *it really is God Who speaks through the person who wrote the words.*

God does not call all of us to be Scripture scholars, but He does expect us to use the means available to better understand His Word to us. If your family were planning a trip, you would probably study maps and possibly even read some books about the area you would be visiting. Studying maps and reading about a region can never take the place of actually making the trip, but it can help you find your way there and also greatly increase your enjoyment of the place when you arrive. In the same way, Bible study aids can keep you from getting lost and increase your understanding. But don't stop there. Try to develop a holy discontent with surface knowledge of Him and keep pressing on to "know Him " as Paul did (Philippians 3:10).

Begin by reading the passage through, referring to your Bible dictionary or commentary if you have any questions about interpretation. If you feel led to do so, follow up by reading the marginal references to related passages of Scripture. You will discover a beautiful network of divinely related concepts. Try to understand the context of the book and the passage as best you can, but don't be so perfectionistic about it that you lose sight of the goal, which is to listen to God. All of these things should be done ahead of time, because you will not be doing any of this study-type work during your time of prayer. In fact, if possible, it's good to do the study part the night before—or, if your Scriptural prayer time is at night, do the

Bible study in the morning, when time allows. In this way, several hours elapse between study and prayer, thus allowing the Word to rise within you in the same way that we set our bread dough aside for a time of rising. Since the passages are short, they will usually not require a great amount of advance study time, and on busy days, this part could immediately precede your prayer time. In fact, if you already have a good understanding of the passage for the day and its context, it's all right to go directly into your prayer period without the preliminary study.

As we become practiced in Scriptural prayer there comes a time when we shift our focus from trying to understand the Bible to trying to listen to God speak to us through it.

THE PRAYER TIME

Once you have completed your study of the passage and are ready for prayer, set aside all ponderings of meaning, all questions you can't answer, all issues you can't solve. If these things are matters about which the Lord wishes to speak to you at this time, the Holy Spirit will clarify their meanings for you. I'll say more about the role of the Holy Spirit in Scriptural prayer in the latter part of this chapter and also in the theme thoughts that precede the Scriptures for Week 29.

Now we are ready to talk about the "wee bit pattern" involved in preparing the soil of your mind so that you can actually hear God speaking to you through His Word. Remember Jesus' parable of the sower? (Mark 4:3–20). In verse 20, He explains that "these are they which are sown on good ground; such as hear the word, and receive it, and bring forth fruit, some thirtyfold, some sixty, and some an hundred." Here are some suggestions to help you cultivate the soil of your mind so that His Word will fall on good ground within you.

1. If you're feeling tense, if it is early and you have just been asleep, or if you've been sitting most of the day, do just a bit of mild physical exercise (toe-touching, arm-swinging, or whatever you like to do). This will help you to relax and keep you from becoming restless during your prayer time.

2. Sit down, take three long, slow, deep breaths, and offer yourself to the Lord, asking Him to speak in you, through His holy Word. If you are preoccupied with problems or worries, bring them to God, lay them at His feet, and let go of them, trusting that, as the Psalmist says, "The Lord will perfect that which concernth me" (Psalm 138:8). Ask forgiveness for your sinfulness and accept that forgiveness, releasing any feelings of guilt you may have been harboring. Ask Him to remove any preconceived ideas you may have about this particular portion of Scripture. This will allow Him to speak to you through it in fresh and overturning ways. Ask God to take charge of your mind during the prayer time, so that all you hear will be truth. Invite the Holy Spirit to be your teacher, claiming Jesus' promise that the Holy Spirit would "teach you all things" (John 14:26).

3. Consider the theme for the week, find the day's Scripture passage, and begin to read, expecting to hear some specific message intended only for you. As you begin your time of Scriptural prayer, remind yourself that what you are reading is written to you and about you. Read the words of Jesus as personally spoken to you. It helps to go so far as to insert your name before you read a sentence spoken by Him. For example, "Bill Smith, the water I shall give ... [you] shall be in ... [you] a well of water springing up into everlasting life" (John 4:14). Try to read Paul's letters as if they came in an envelope addressed to you and arrived in today's mail. Read aloud, if possible. If you're embarrassed to do that because others are within

hearing distance, whisper it, or at least move your lips as you read the words. This helps to imprint them more deeply in your mind.

Read very slowly, letting each word resonate within you. You may find this hard to do at first. We live in an age in which everything is shifted into high gear. Speed-reading courses have convinced us that faster is better. But in praying with Scripture, it's important to listen with the heart instead of with the mind. You will not hear God speaking to you unless you learn to savor the Word, to let it resound within you, to let it soothe and fill your hungry spirit, like fine home-baked bread. Read a word or two and then pause, letting it hover over your spirit like a bird resting on the wind.

4. Continue in this way until our Lord stops you (and He will!). When you feel moved in some way—lifted in spirit, filled with peace, aware of God's love flowing through you, strengthened in faith, *pause*, and just rest in His grace and presence. Do not mar this moment with words, for within its space lies the healing, the restoration, the atonement (at-one-ment). When you gaze at a great work of art, you don't give it a hurried glance and say, "That's a beach scene," as you walk toward the next painting. You stand in front of it and let its beauty soak into you until it begins to resonate within your heart. Allow the Word of God to penetrate your being in the same way. If you read all the way through the passage without being stopped, that's o.k. Just begin again. Eventually, He will stop you. Once, I read through a short portion of Scripture fourteen times without any inner response at all. Then, on that fifteenth reading, it seemed as if the sky split open, and a *life-changing* insight burst upon my stunned awareness.

You'll be amazed at how frequently the Lord will speak very specifically to your very needs. This really became evident to me at a retreat in which I was leading the group into Scriptural prayer. I had explained the procedure, given them the passage in Acts that tells about Paul and Silas singing praises to the Lord while they were chained in prison (Acts 16:25–34), and sent them off to their rooms to pray with this Scripture. Then we all came back and shared what God had said to us during our prayer time. One lady said, "I've been feeling so tied down, caring for my mother-in-law, who is an invalid. But as I prayed with this Scripture, I suddenly realized that *I can sing in my chains!* He reminded me that my freedom is always there, because I can be lifted out of bondage by singing and praising Him! I love to play the piano and sing, but I've been feeling so burdened I haven't done it for a long time. I'm so thankful to the Lord for showing me this way back to freedom."

Another lady began to cry as she told about what the Lord had said to her in the same verses. "He showed me just how deeply imprisoned I've become. There's something in my life that I've been denying for a long time. My husband and my parents and even my grown children have been trying to convince me to get help, but I wouldn't admit I needed it. But it was so clear today, when the Lord spoke to me through His Word. I knew I couldn't fool myself any longer. I'm going to get in touch with Alcoholics Anonymous."

This sort of thing happens time after time when I teach this method of prayer to a group. Obviously, it isn't a question of interpretation. It's just that God can use the same passage to speak personally to each individual.

5. After the Lord has stopped you and you have allowed enough silence for the Word to germinate within you, then begin to talk with Him in response to this movement of Grace. Ask Him why He stopped you at this particular place. You may want to ask Him a question

about the passage, or to praise Him for what you have just experienced, or to ask Him to help you to continue in fellowship with Him. Just tell Him whatever is on your heart. Then pause again and wait for His further response. You may hold this conversation silently, in your mind, but I've found that when I do that, my mind tends to wander. To avoid this, either speak out loud, or write your conversation with the Lord in your notebook as it is happening. You'll be surprised at how easily it flows, once you get started! Continue in this way for as long as you feel led to do so. Then begin reading again, slowly.

You ought not to stop reading the Word until you feel happy in God; then you will feel fit to go out to your day's work. Day by day, our Lord will reveal to you more of Himself and of His teaching. Fresh new insights will begin to shine in you like stars in the heavens. He will gradually come alive in you, so that eventually you may be able to say, with Paul, "I live; yet not I, but Christ liveth in me" (Galatians 2:20).

6. At the end of your prayer period, choose a word or phrase from all that He has said, either in the Scripture passage or in your conversation with Him. This will be His special gift to you for the next twenty-four hours—a reminder of His real presence in your life, something to ponder and to savor and to live by until your next meeting with Him. Like the psalmist, tuck the Word deep down in your heart (Psalm 119:11). Some days, you'll know exactly which word(s) He wants you to take. Other days, you'll need to make a deliberate choice.

7. Conclude with a short prayer of thanksgiving for this Person-to-person communication you have just experienced. Sometimes your heart will be so full, praise will break forth spontaneously.

8. Record in your spiritual journal (that notebook we mentioned earlier) the significant movements of the prayer

period. Be sure to mark the date, the book, chapter, and verses you read and copy down any words or verses in which you felt Him speaking directly to you. Include Bible verses that struck you afresh, emotions you felt, insights you received, and whatever else seems important to you. You may want to write down your special word(s) for the day and carry them with you on a small card or slip of paper.

PREVENTIVE MAINTENANCE

My husband takes care of my car for me, getting the oil changed, the engine greased, and minor repairs done on a regular basis. He calls this "preventive maintenance," and I'm sure it's largely responsible for the fact that my car has remained trouble-free during the eight years I've owned it.

By way of preventive maintenance, I'm going to mention a few problems that may or may not arise as you begin praying with your Bible, and give you some suggestions for dealing with them, in order to keep your daily time with the Lord in His Word running smoothly.

1. *Avoidance.* Most of the time, you'll find this type of prayer so rewarding that you'll look forward to your daily date with the Lord with the kind of eagerness you have when you're expecting an important letter from someone you love. But I should also warn you that there will be times when you'll find yourself making excuses. "I've just got too much to do today." Or "I can't pray with my Bible today because we have house guests." Or "I'm just too tired." At times like these, be gentle but firm with yourself. Reduce your time if you must, but don't stand God up. Even on the busiest day, you can carve out five or ten minutes for Him, and that's far better than breaking your commitment by "skipping it just this once."

2. *Dryness.* There will also be periods of dryness in your Scriptural prayer, and it's important for you to realize that these, too, are movements of the Lord, planned by Him for your growth in faith. In fact, if you have been faithful to your commitment to the Lord, a dry period is a pretty sure sign that the Holy Spirit is working quietly, imperceptibly, within you! If you've ever tried to burn leaves in the fall, you know that the drier they are, the more gloriously they flame up. When God dries the leaves of your soul, remind yourself He is making it ready to receive, anew, the flaming grace of His Holy Spirit.

3. *Nothing happening.* If you think nothing is happening, ask yourself what that "nothing" is. You may be experiencing some negative emotion you'd rather not face, or you may have started daydreaming, or worrying. Acknowledging what is really happening may lead you to new insight and help you to relinquish whatever is blocking you. Just give it to God. Then you will be able to refocus on your prayer.

4. *Fear.* Once in a while, especially if the Lord wants to speak to you about something in your past that He wishes to help you resolve, it's possible that you may encounter some feelings of fearfulness. If this should occur, immediately visualize Jesus standing by your side. Ask Him to guide you and to handle any situation that seems threatening to you. He will *never* confront you with anything you're not ready to handle, with His help. He will say to your inner storm, "Peace, be still" (Mark 4:39) and you will then begin to feel a calming of any emotional turmoil, and peace will return. There's a bonus, here, because you will find yourself calling up a mental picture of Jesus when actual fear situations arise in your daily life, too![3]

5. *Clock-watching.* If you find that, because you've agreed to spend a certain amount of time with the Lord, you are

frequently interrupting your prayer to look at your watch, it will be helpful to set a timer so you won't have to think about time. If it's one that ticks, better put it in the next room.

6. *Falling asleep.* If you often fall asleep during your Scriptural prayer time, please look for a reason. The most obvious one is that you may not be getting enough sleep and are simply tired. Or you may have scheduled your prayer for a time when your body is at a low. These things should be faced and worked out. On the other hand, you may fall asleep because you really don't want to face what God is saying to you at this time. Sometimes the voice of the Lord will be gentle, consoling. At other times it may be that of a Father Who cares enough about His child to be firm—a voice that points out areas in which the child needs to grow and change. If you think this may apply to you, ask yourself these questions:

a. Is there a warning here for me?
b. Am I guilty of the same kind of sin that's exposed in the passage?
c. Is there a difficult example the Lord is calling me to follow?
d. Is there a job He wants me to do that I'd rather avoid?
e. Is He asking me to change my lifestyle or value system?
f. Does He want me to rearrange my priorities?
g. Do I need to change my attitude about something?

These questions should be considered, not only if falling asleep is a problem, but any time you feel resistance to the Scripture or to your prayer time.

SUMMARY

So, briefly, the procedure is:

A. Before Prayer Time
   1. Make a prayer covenant.
   2. Establish a regular place for prayer.
   3. Minimize distractions.
   4. Assemble materials.
   5. Locate the passage for the day.

B. At Prayer Time
   1. Do some mild physical exercise.
   2. Ask the Lord to speak in you.
   3. Read slowly, listening with your heart.
   4. Read until He stops you.
   5. Rest in His presence.
   6. Converse with the Lord in response.
   7. Choose a word or phrase to take away.
   8. Offer a short prayer of thanksgiving.
   9. Record significant movements in your journal.

Just as the disciples felt their hearts burn within them on the road to Emmaus as the risen Christ opened the Scriptures to them (Luke 24:32), *your* eyes and heart will be opened to His presence in ways you may never have known before, as you pray with your Bible. Jesus stands by your side at this moment, ready to make Himself known to you through His Word. He does this by the Holy Spirit, and you can rely on Him completely to guide your prayer and to make that Word come alive within you. The Holy Spirit gives the Word its light and power and keeps you in blessed childlike openness. Let us praise God for this astounding gift of the Holy Spirit, and let us look with awakened hope and anticipation to a new and more intimate relationship with our precious Lord and loving Friend, Jesus Christ.

NOTES

1. A version of the suggestions given in items 1–3 originally appeared in my *Guideposts* article in the May, 1982, issue of that magazine.

2. George Martin, *Reading Scripture as the Word of God* (Ann Arbor, Mich.: Servant Books, 1975), p. 5.

3. If fear during Scriptural prayer is a real problem for you, please turn, now, to the material given for Week 29.

PART III

Themes
and Scriptures
for Thirty Weeks

Week 1
"I invite you"

Do you remember the thrill of being invited to a birthday party when you were a child—or the chosen-ness you felt when you were invited to join a club, or the excitement of being singled out by that special boy or girl, for your first date? Try to think back to some moment in your life when you knew the joy of being invited, the thrill of being chosen. Spend a few minutes, right now, re-living that moment.

Sometime during this first week of listening to God as you pray with the Bible, your heart will hear Him say to you something like this: "I have chosen you. By implanting within you a hunger for prayer, I am calling you to a deeper relationship of love with Me. I want you to come so I can heal you, so I can fill you with My peace and give you rest. If you feel unworthy, I will cleanse you and make you free to respond to My invitation. If you feel rejected by the world, I will bind up your wounds and wrap you in My love. Come to me." Be open and you *will* be invited.

To give you an idea of how the conversational part of

Scriptural prayer works, I'll quote a few lines of dialogue from my journal, written during my first week of praying with the Scriptures. The Scripture is Isaiah 6:1–13. I wrote:

> The Lord stopped me at verse 13 today: "... as a teil tree, and as an oak, whose substance is in them, when they cast their leaves: so the holy seed shall be the substance thereof."
>
> "What do you want to say to me in this Scripture, Lord?"
>
> "Throw off all unnecessary things, and the Substance, which is Myself, will remain, and grow, and feed you."
>
> "What things do you want me to eliminate, Lord?"
>
> "When you come to Me, put away all your worries and cares, let go of all thoughts, be unattached to worldly things. Just love Me and I will give you all of Myself."
>
> "It's so hard for me to get my mind off of my daily problems, Lord, so I can center myself in You. Please help me to do this!"
>
> "Just offer Me your willing heart, and I will do the rest."
>
> "I feel suddenly released from the burden of having to do it all myself. Praise You, Lord. I feel Your nearness. Thank You for calling me, and thank You even more for helping me to answer Your call."

The Lord our God is calling *you*. He will not speak to you in exactly the same way He speaks to me, but as you read the daily Scriptures, He will open the ears of your heart. Your name is on His invitation list. Please receive and accept that bid.   •

Texts for Week 1

Isaiah 55. Invitation to Grace.

I Samuel 3:1–10. The call of Samuel.

Revelation 3:14–22. He knocks at your door.

Mark 6:30–44. "Come apart and rest with Me."

Psalm 95. How to hear His voice.

Matthew 11:25–30. Jesus invites you to come to Him with your burdens and anxieties.

Isaiah 6:1–10. Call of Isaiah. God awaits *your* response: "Here I am."

Week 2
"I want to speak to you through My Word"

I don't know what your Bible background is, but I might as well admit something to you right at the beginning. Until about four years ago, the Bible reading that I did was not very rewarding. I grew up in a church that didn't particularly encourage personal Bible reading, so spending time in the Word did not come naturally for me. Then I attended a Scriptural prayer retreat at the Crosier Renewal Center in Hastings, Nebraska, directed by Father Joseph Smerke, O.S.C., and for the first time, I heard the Lord speak directly and personally to me through His Word. He has been doing just that every day since then, and this daily experience of His *actual presence* within the Word has transformed my life.

Praying with Scripture is the most exciting thing I do because it involves me in the great mystery of God communicating with me. He can take *any* Bible passage and use it to speak to my specific concerns of the moment, no matter what they are. I know this because He has done it over and over again. You'll be reading about some of these incidents in the following pages.

So come to your prayer time this week with an expectant faith, a faith that believes in the transforming power of His holy Word for your life. Come before God ready to receive from Him whatever He wills to give or say to you. If He seems to be speaking to you about something that has nothing whatever to do with the theme for the week, that's o.k. Don't fight it. He knows what you need to hear and what He wants to say to you at this moment of your life. Read the Word as His love letter to you, and you will find that the Bible contains not only His message to you but also His very Presence.

Texts for Week 2

Isaiah 55:1–3, 10,11. The Word of God is divine food prepared for you.

Romans 10:8–17. The Word is on your lips, in your heart.

Mark 4:1–20. Jesus invites you to listen to Him.

Psalm 8. The majesty of God, the dignity of man.

Psalm 19. His words are sweeter than honey.

John 1:1–14. The Word was made flesh.

James 1:17–25. Be doers of the word.

Week 3
"I love you with a creating love"

Our daughter, Karen, is majoring in art in college. Not long ago, as she was working on a self-portrait, her fourteen-year-old brother John said, "Who's *that* supposed to be?" When she told him, he said, "But it doesn't look like you!"

"That's because I'm not done with it yet. You just wait. By the time I'm ready to hand it in, you'll see that it looks just like me."

Karen was right. The painting did look very much like her when it was done.

When we read in the Bible that God created us in His

own image, the question naturally arises, "Then why are we so flawed?" Of course, that question could be answered in terms of man's fall from Grace through Adam. But I think there's another factor involved, and that is the fact that God is still creating us. Every moment of every day, He is creating me anew. When I was born, He breathed into my nostrils the breath of life, and I became a living soul. With every breath I take, He continues to love life into me.

Did you know that in both the Old Testament and the New Testament, the word that is used for *breath* is the same word that is used for *spirit*? In fact, in the early translations, Holy Spirit was translated as Holy Breath. So this week, as you focus on God's creating love, try to become aware of your breath as the gift of Life that God is pouring out upon you every minute of your earthly existence.

Begin your prayer sessions this week by taking a few minutes to breathe deeply. My friend, Alice, taught me a breating exercise called the "Holy Breath," that has done wonders for me, physically as well as spiritually. Here's how it is done: Place your hand on a pulse center, either in your wrist or throat, and begin counting the beats. Inhale slowly, for the count of seven heartbeats, being aware of the fact that you are *breathing in Spirit*. Hold the breath just long enough to say silently, in your heart, "The kingdom of God is within . . . [me]" (Luke 17:21). Then exhale slowly, for a count of seven heartbeats. Repeat this seven times. You'll be amazed at how relaxed you'll feel and open to the creating love of God.

Texts for Week 3

Genesis 1:26–28, 2:4–7. God creates you, gives you the breath of life.

Isaiah 43:1–7. God calls you by name, tells you you are precious.

Psalm 104:24–34. God pours out His riches for you.

Isaiah 49:1–16 (especially 1–2, 14–16). The Lord called you before you were born.

Psalm 100. Stand in awe of His creating love.

Isaiah 54:1–10. God's love for you can never be shaken.

John 15:1–11. Jesus proclaims the constancy of His love for you.

Week 4
"I love you with a providing and caring love"

Several years ago, there was an article in *Guideposts* magazine by Bill Burke, who invented seat-lift recliner chairs for invalids. Four years after he started manufacturing the chairs, his life savings were gone, his home was mortgaged, and he had borrowed to the hilt on his life insurance. He owed nineteen months rent on the little frame building where the chairs were made, $30,000.00 to the bank, and hundreds of dollars more in unpaid bills. Bill and Zella sat at their kitchen table, pouring over their bills and counting their assets. Between the two of them, they had just a little over $2.00. Bill buried his head in his hands and said, "I can't go on anymore. I give up."

But Zella put her arms around him and said, "Oh no you don't, Bill Burke. God gave you the ability to invent and showed you how to use that talent to help sick people. Maybe we've been trying too hard to do it all ourselves— not really trusting the Lord. Let's turn it all over to Him and listen and do what He tells us to do." So the Burkes got down on their knees in their mortgaged house and Bill prayed, "Lord, I have to confess that I haven't trusted You enough. But right now I'm turning the whole business over to You. From now on You're the Boss. Just let us know how to run Your business."

The next morning, Bill woke with these words floating

across his mind: "Show your trust in the Lord by trusting other people." Bill acted on that advice by deciding to ship chairs to anyone who needed them, paying all the freight, without checking the people's credit, letting them pay only if the chairs really helped them. Miraculously, the bank stood behind Bill, covering complete expenses for every chair he got somebody to try.

Bill says that "Once we made the Lord our Boss He developed more products, solved our financial problems, and directed our 'trust people' sales philosophy. We now have 30 employees, two-thirds of whom are handicapped and/or over 50 (Boss's orders), and our business volume has exceeded my wildest dreams—all because we turned the whole thing over to Him, trusting Him to provide."[1]

No matter what your needs are, let this be the week that you turn them all over to God. Make Him the Boss in your life and affairs, and *He will provide*. If you find it difficult to let go and relinquish your problems, let Him help you to do it, as He speaks to you through this week's Bible texts.

Texts for Week 4

Psalm 23. God cares and provides.

Luke 12:22–32. Don't worry about tomorrow. God is a loving Father Who supplies all your needs.

Psalm 91. You can trust Him.

Jeremiah 29:11–14. Our Lord has plans for you.

Psalm 27. There is nothing to fear. He keeps you safe.

Ephesians 2:1–10. God gives you riches in grace and kindness.

Psalm 34. Praise God, Who loves you so much.

NOTES

1. Bill Burke, "Who's Boss Around Here?" *Guideposts*, September 1979, pp. 10–13.

Week 5
"Do not be discouraged"

There is an old saying: "Give me the place to stand and a lever long enough and I will move the world." It is true that a lever can move things that couldn't be budged any other way. There are things that you and I couldn't possibly lift by our own strength that we can handle easily by using the principle of leverage.

I need to remember that principle when I feel weak and helpless, when I face seemingly impossible situations in my life, because, as a Christian, I have access to a spiritual lever. The lever is prayer and it's up to me to provide that part, but Christ gives me the place to stand. A lever by itself is just a rod; a prayer that leaves out Christ is powerless. But, oh, the mighty force for good that can be exerted when the lever of prayer is combined with the strength of Jesus' name!

Are you facing some overwhelming task? Or is there an impossible situation in your life, something you've given up on? If so, pray about it in Jesus' name. Then form a mental picture of your burden being lifted by the lever of prayer and the power of Jesus' name. Whenever you feel discouraged, recall this picture, mentally place your problem or task on the end of the lever, and call on the name of Jesus. You'll be surprised at the mighty forces that will come to your aid!

Move mountains? You and I? Why not!

Texts for Week 5
John 14:9–14. Ask in His name, and He will do it.

Mark 11:22–26. You can move mountains.
Philippians 4:8–13. He will make you able to do all things.
Isaiah 40:28–31. Feel Him lifting you.
Psalm 62. The Lord is your rock and your defense.
Habakkuk 3:17–19. No matter how bad things get, He will
  see you through.
Psalm 121. The Lord is your help in all things.

Week 6
Listen to God's answer to your sinfulness:
"I love you, anyway!"

I know a lady who ended up in a mental hospital because
she was raised by parents who constantly reminded her
of her own sinfulness. "God is watching you," they'd say,
"And the devil's after you. You'll pay for what you've
done!" By midlife, she was seeing Satan everywhere and
living in a state of constant fear.

We need to be aware of our sinfulness in order to repent. But I'm quite sure that God didn't intend for us to
wallow in feelings of unworthiness or carry around great
huge burdens of guilt. Self-debasement is unhealthy, not
only mentally and physically, but also spiritually.

Over and over in the Bible, we see God's disappointment about man's sinfulness. Sin is a tragic rejection of
God's love and yet, our heavenly Father loves us so much
that He keeps calling us back. If we refuse to accept His
forgiveness, we refuse to accept His greatest gift to us—
His Son, Jesus Christ. Because of Him, we never need to
carry our guilt from one day into the next.

An old man recently told me about an incident from his
school days. A group of boys had been making life miser-
able for their young teacher—tacks on her chair, frogs in
the wastebasket, spitwads shooting across the room, graffiti
scratched into desks. So one day, the teacher listed all of

the offenses on the blackboard and said, "Now I already know who did each of these, but for *your* sakes, it's important that you confess and apologize. I'm going to be in the classroom during both recesses today and also after school. If anyone wants to admit anything and apologize, I'll simply erase that offense from the board and forget about it. Any items still on the board tomorrow will be reported to your parents." By the end of the day the board was wiped clean.

Like that teacher, Jesus already knows what my sins are. It's just that it's sometimes hard for me to believe that He really does erase them, once I've repented and asked forgiveness.

As you read this week's Scriptures, let yourself experience the forgiving love of God, through Christ. If you have trouble accepting His total forgiveness, here's a visualization that may help to convince your heart. Before you go to bed tonight, write the day's sins on a blackboard in your mind's eye. Then go down the list and, as you ask Jesus to forgive you for each one, see Him erasing that offense from your soul's blackboard. Then give thanks and start afresh.

Texts for Week 6

Hosea 2:14–23. God welcomes His unfaithful beloved, Israel, with all the fervor of His first love and showers gifts on her. (Remember, as you're praying with this Scripture, that Israel represents *you*.)

Joel 2:12–17. God calls you to repentance.

Psalm 32. Confession and admission of sin bring healing forgiveness from God.

Luke 15:1–7. Parable of the lost sheep.

Psalm 103. God is love; He forgives all; He overlooks your faults so you can repent.

John 10:1–18. The Good Shepherd.

Luke 15:11–32. Parable of the Prodigal Son.

Week 7
"I want you to be happy"[1]

If you had an infection in your body, you surely wouldn't take arsenic to heal yourself. Yet most of us do the mental equivalent of that every time a problem arises in our lives. We drink in spiritual poison, and the name of that poison is worry.

One day last winter, I visited a man who was in the hospital suffering from a severe attack of colitis. He told me that the doctor had said that worry was literally eating him up inside and he knew the doctor was right. But then he said, "I just can't help it. I know worry doesn't do any good, but just knowing that doesn't help me stop doing it."

I think this patient had a good point. We can't just *decide* not to worry. We need an antidote, something to neutralize the poison. One of the most effective antidotes to worry that I've found is walking prayer. Not only is it good worry therapy, but it also helps in coping with other kinds of negative emotions that we all have at times: anger, fear, jealousy, grief, resentment, guilt, loneliness, worry, self-pity, and all those other robbers of our serenity.

So this week, you may want to try walking prayer as a part of your time spent with the Lord. In fact, it's a form of Scriptural prayer that you may choose to do with any of the weekly themes—not just this one. Here's how it works:

1. Choose a short verse (or even just a word or phrase) from the day's Bible reading—one that really speaks to you.

2. Then take a walk with our Lord. It's best to go alone, but if you decide to walk with someone, agree not to talk.

Then, as you walk, just begin repeating the passage over and over in your mind. Don't strain; let the words flow lightly and easily through your consciousness. If your mind wanders (and it probably will) don't become upset. Just gently bring it back to your prayer verse and begin again.

3. Continue your walk for at least ten minutes or longer.

Walking prayer "may not solve your problem for you," but it will help you to see the situation in God's light. It will also generate spiritual strength, which will help you to cope with your problem more effectively. "Also, beccause it focuses your mind on God instead of on your worry, it is very likely to give you a whole new perspective on your problem."[2]

Texts for Week 7

Psalm 51:1–12. If you're feeling guilty, He will cleanse you.

John 14:18–27. He will comfort you.

Isaiah 40:28–31. When you are tired or impatient or sick, He will restore you.

Romans 8:31–39. Even if you feel friendless, you are never alone.

Philippians 4:6–13. When you lack confidence, He will be your strength.

Psalm 30. He will turn your sadness into dancing.

Psalm 147:1–14. When you feel hurt or rejected, the Lord will soothe you.

NOTES

1. Portions of this section on walking prayer are taken from my book, *Beyond TM: A Practical Guide to the Lost Traditions of*

Christian Meditation (Ramsey, N.J.: Paulist Press, 1980), which also offers further suggestions for coping with worry and other negative emotions.

2. In the Appendix, I have provided a list of Scripture passages chosen to help you cope with specific emotional problems and situations, with the help of walking prayer.

Week 8
"Do not be afraid. I will protect you"

Last week, we talked about worry and admitted that we can't just *decide* not to do it. Walking prayer is a way to wash away the poison of worry. It is also a good antidote for fear, but there are times when it is neither convenient nor expedient for us to walk. There are those moments of panic that strike just as you are about to give a public talk, or when it's 3:00 A.M. and your teenager isn't home yet, or while waiting for someone to come out of surgery.

There's a Scripture passage that has helped me through many such situations. It's Isaiah 43:2—"When thou passest through the waters, I will be with thee; and through the rivers, they shall not overflow thee." Maybe the reason this means so much to me is because of something that happened to me when I was about ten years old. My dad and brother and I were on a fishing trip in a backwoods area of the Rockies. We had to cross a fast-moving stream by walking on a narrow log for ten to twelve feet, and I was afraid of falling into the icy waters. Daddy told me not to look at the log or the water but to pick a spot on the other bank and picture myself already there. "Just throw your mind across," he said, "and your feet will follow."

I do quite a bit of public speaking, and sometimes stage fright strikes when I least expect it. When that happens, I've learned to "throw my mind across" by first claiming God's promise from Isaiah and then picturing myself standing in front of the group and delivering my speech with poise and confidence. My fearfulness always disappears when I do this.

What kinds of fears are you subject to? Submit them to the Lord this week, as you pray with His words of reassurance and protection. Maybe He will give you a short sentence or phrase that will help you to "throw your mind across" to safety, when you face frightening situations. If so, memorize it, hold onto it, let it be your lifeline. When fear strikes, refuse to think of any negative outcome. Instead, picture, as vividly as you possibly can, the working out of God's perfection.

Texts for Week 8

Joshua 1:1–9. God's promise to be with you, wherever you go.

Isaiah 26:1–4. Keep your mind on Him and He will keep you safe.

Psalm 27. With the Lord on your side, nothing can harm you.

Isaiah 43:1–7. You are called by His name. He will stay with you always.

Romans 8:28–39. Nothing can separate you from God's loving care.

Psalm 23. He takes care of His sheep.

Psalm 56. When you are afraid, you can trust in Him.

Week 9
*"When you have too much to do,
I will help you accomplish it"*

Little did I guess, when I asked the Lord to use me, that He would put me to work leading four prayer retreats in three different cities—all in the shortest month of the year. "I'm not complaining," I said to my friend Judy.

"It's just that I'm not sure I'll have the energy to do justice to all of this." Judy spends many hours each week praying with and counseling troubled Christians, so I asked her, "How in the world do you keep on top of it all? What's your secret?"

Judy told me her secret, and it's a powerhouse. She said, "I just keep reminding myself, several times a day that, since the Lord gave me this work, *He* will see it through for me. There's a passage in Job that really helps me with this. It's 'He performeth the thing that is appointed for me' (Job 23:14). Each morning when I get up, I say it over and over in my mind—as I'm getting dressed, while I'm brushing my teeth, driving to work, and while I'm working. Before I meet with each person, I repeat those words, trusting Him every minute to do His work through me. And He does!"

My first February retreat was only a week away when I talked to Judy. I started right in using the affirmation from Job every day, and I felt confident that He would carry the work through for me successfully. And He did.

If the Lord has given you a ministry (and He does give assignments to all who ask), this week's Scriptures can help you to know, deep inside, that He will help you to complete it.

Texts for Week 9

Philippians 4:9–13. You can do all things.
Matthew 11:28–30. The easy way.
II Peter 1:4–10. How to succeed.
Psalm 28:6–9. He is your strength.
Psalm 40:1–5. He does wonderful works through you.
Isaiah 45:1–4. He will smooth a path for you.
Job 23:10–14. Let Him do it for you.

Week 10
"I will guide your decisions"

I've made an astounding discovery. Since I've been praying with my Bible, I've found that the Lord can use *whatever* passage I'm praying with to speak to me about my specific situation at the time. I discovered this a while back, when I had a really tough decision to make. It was one of those situations for which there seemed to be no good solution, and no matter which way I decided, somebody was going to be mad at me. My Scripture reading for the day was Psalm 138, which is a song of praise and reassurance. I remember thinking, "what I need today is guidance, not reassurance." But I asked God to use the Scripture to help me with my decision, anyway.

He stopped me at verse 8: "The Lord will perfect that which concerneth me." I began a dialogue with God in my notebook. "That's comforting, Lord, but it doesn't help me with my decision. Show me how to use it."

God seemed to reply: "Pray for direction, and then use that verse as an affirmation."

"How am I to do that, Lord?"

"Throughout the day, whenever you think about your problem situation, just mentally repeat those words of the Psalm, letting their meaning permeate your consciousness. Then let go, leaving your mind open and clear, without trying to force an answer."

"Will you guide me then, God?"

"Why don't you try it and see?"

I did just that, and to my astonishment, that evening as I was doing the dinner dishes, an idea flashed into my mind. I saw the problem from another perspective and realized that it wasn't an either/or situation, after all. A combination solution was called for, and it would be acceptable to all concerned. Since then, I've used this method of listening for God's guidance in many different decisions, and it has never failed to bring a satisfactory answer. Sometimes it comes as a sudden flash of insight, a deep inner knowing. At other times, it rises up through my unconscious mind as I'm doing some mundane task. It may leap from the page of a book I'm reading or flash into my mind as I'm falling asleep. It may not come for several days, but I've learned that if I continue to affirm God's perfection in regard to the situation, His perfect guidance always comes.

The Scripture readings for this week will help you to tune in to God's guidance. But there's always the question, "How can I be sure it's really God's answer and not just my own will?" I've learned that, if the guidance is really from Him, He'll send confirmation from another direction, if I keep open and watch and listen. It may be a new development in a prayed-about situation; sometimes it's an image that floats across my mind as I'm falling asleep. Or it may be a supporting word from a trusted friend. So when you're in doubt about whether or not your guidance is from the Lord, wait attentively for a confirmation. When the same answer comes through more than one channel and you feel the lines intersecting within your soul, you can then plot your course with assurance.

Texts for Week 10

Psalm 25. Calling on God to show you the way.
Isaiah 30:18–21. His promise of guidance.
Proverbs 8:1–14. "I am understanding."
Luke 11:9–13. "Ask, and it shall be given you."
Psalm 73:11–24. He will give you counsel.
John 9:1–11. He will help you to see.
Psalm 138. "The Lord will perfect that which concerneth me."

Week 11
"Prepare ye the way"

Isaiah prophesied that God would send a messenger to prepare the way of the Lord. That messenger was John the Baptist. But did you know that *you* are also the fulfillment of that prophecy? Even at this very moment, God is calling you to prepare the way for the coming of His Son. He wants Christ to be born anew in your heart. John the Baptist is our guide for preparing the way. Let's look at seven Scripture passages that describe his preparations. Realize, as you pray with these verses, that they are spoken directly to you. Think of this week's Scriptural prayer as a pilgrimage.

To make straight His path, you'll need to clear a space in the wilderness of your life, overgrown as it is with work, family, social activities, and the many other things that take up your time. You have already begun that task by setting aside daily time for being alone with God.

Next, John the Baptist urges you to repent. Examine your soul. Pray for a spirit of repentance. Confess your sins to God. Ask your heavenly Father to wash away your guilt, bring light to your thoughts, and purify your motives. You may decide to perform some tangible act as evidence of your repentance, such as reaffirming your Baptismal vows or finding some person you've wronged and making things right within him.

On the third day, as you read about John's doubts, search your own mind and heart. Try to recognize any doubts that may be lurking there. Admit them and bring them to Jesus for healing.

On the fourth day, consider John's answer to those who asked what they must do to be ready for the coming of the Messiah. His answer is for you, too. What could you spare? What would you share? Look through your closets, your drawers, your pantry, your purse. Then discover the joy of sharing with those less fortunate.

On the fifth day, as you pray with the two Scriptures, decide what the Lord is asking of *you*, in order to fulfill this prophesy. Then make a sincere effort to heal any wounded relationships in your family.

On the sixth day, consider what you might do to ensure that He will increase and you will decrease. If there are people who look to you for spiritual help, point their eyes away from you to Him. Are there any ways in which you are accepting glory you could be giving to Him?

Finally, on the last day of the week, invite the Christ Child into your carefully prepared heart. Maybe you'll want to make a ceremony of it by lighting a candle or two and making a special offering. He calls you now, and for the rest of your life, to be His home in the world, to bear His name, to mirror His presence in the world.

Texts for Week 11

Isaiah 40:1–11. The prophecy.

Matthew 3:1–6. John the Baptist preaches repentance.

Matthew 11:1–6. John admits his doubts and asks Jesus for reassurance.

Luke 3:1–11. John answers the question, "What shall we do to be ready for the Lord?"

Malachi 4:6 and Luke 1:17. Healing wounded relationships in preparation for His coming.

John 3:25–36. What is your relationship with Christ?

John 3:6–21. Let Christ be born in your heart.

Week 12

"I give you My Son"

My grandmother Banta used to tell us children a story about a beautiful angel named Amiah who went around every year, just before Christmas, looking for the perfect birthplace for the Baby Jesus. Amiah wasn't looking for a palace or a church or even a manger. She was looking for a warm and loving human heart. Grandmother said *that* was the perfect birthplace for God's Son.

Even now, I'm awe-struck by the thought that God loves me so much that He wants His Son to become incarnate in my heart. But it's true! In the person of Jesus, God spoke Himself into humanity, and when I pray with the New Testament, I can actually make contact with the living presence of Christ, abiding within me (John 14:20). One way of doing this is by spiritually entering into a Scriptural scene, to be present with my Friend, Jesus, in order that I may know Him better and love Him more deeply.

This is a simple, freeing kind of prayer that's very likely to astound you with the dynamic livingness of Christ's presence in this eternal now. It has two movements.

1. After you have read the passage several times, place yourself in the scene, either as an observer or as one of the persons mentioned in the text. Now look around. Is it day or night? Warm or cold? What background sights do you see? What sounds and smells do you sense? Who are the people there? How are they dressed? What expressions are on their faces? Now, you don't have to research all these details. This is prayer, not scholarship. Let the Holy Spirit help set the scene in your mind.

2. Once you are part of the scene, just let go and allow the second movement to begin: Jesus Christ will present Himself to you in the incident you are contemplating. When this happens, begin to interact with Him and with others in the scene, as the Spirit directs. That's all there is to it.

This prayer is for real. True, it *begins* with your human imagination, but at some point it goes beyond that, as the

Spirit draws you into the mystery of Christ's presence. At times, you may be carried beyond the externals to an experience of events not recorded in the text but meant especially for you at this particular moment of your life. You may find yourself crying . . . or laughing. You may feel moved to pick up that Baby from His manger bed, holding Him, rocking Him in your arms, adoring Him in ways beyond any prayer you've experienced before. You may feel led to take Mary and Joseph into your own home when they are told there's no room at the inn. What indescribable joy you may experience.

Now, don't let your logic-fettered rational mind get in the way by saying, "But that wasn't the way it really happened." Of course not. And you know that. But if this is what happens in your prayer, it is what the Lord wants you to experience now, so that He may become more alive and real within you. So just relax into the scene and let it happen. You are in the arms of the Holy Spirit, Who prays within you.

Entering scenes from the Bible is just another way of praying with Scripture. Sometimes you'll want to pray this way and other times you'll prefer to continue as in previous weeks. Throughout the remaining weeks, I'll mark with an asterisk (*) the passages that best lend themselves to this method.

Lord Jesus, as we enter into this new dimension of prayer, we ask for the grace of a more intimate knowledge of You at the very core of our being.

Texts for Week 12

Isaiah 9:6–1. The Messiah will come as a child, have many names, bring peace.

Luke 1:26–28. The startling visitation to Mary; her response.

*Luke 2:1–7. The birth of Jesus.

*Luke 2:8–20. The shepherds hear the joyful news.
John 1:11–18. The Word is made flesh.
Philippians 2:5–11. The humility of Jesus.
*Matthew 2:1–12. Visit and adoration of the Magi.

Week 13
"I was human like you"

Jeanine was a timid, sweet-faced young woman, about thirty, who hadn't said a word since our retreat started. As we came back to our meeting room after spending a private hour praying with the Bible, I noticed that her face, so pale before, had a rosy glow, and her soft brown eyes glistened. We'd been listening to Jesus say, "I was human like you."

I asked for volunteers to begin the sharing time. To my surprise, Jeanine bubbled, "Guess what, girls. I think I've fallen in love!" She had chosen to pray with Matthew 11:25–30. "Verse 29 was the one that got me," she said. "It's: 'for I am meek and lowly in heart.' Although I've read that verse many times, I'd never really thought of Jesus, of *the Christ*, as meek and lowly. To me, God has always been a powerful Being, off in the sky somewhere, watching everything I do, waiting to reward or punish me. My own father was very strict and punitive, so I guess I just assumed God was that way, too. In fact, I've always been kind of afraid of men. But today, as I prayed with just this one verse, I met a man I could relate to. I found out that He's *approachable*. He's tender and gentle, quiet and kind. Just the sort of man I like! I was even able to tell Him I love Him. If you knew me, you'd realize how bold that seems. And this man—this gentle, unassuming man—is also God! It's almost more than I can grasp. I've never really known Jesus before, I guess. Now I feel like a young girl who's fallen in love for the first time!"

It is my prayer that this week you'll become personally acquainted with a very human man named Jesus, that He'll become more real to you than ever before, and that you'll fall in love with Him in new and previously un-dreamed-of ways.

Texts for Week 13

Luke 4:1–13. Jesus knew how temptation feels.

*Matthew 21:10–13. Even the emotion of anger was not beyond Him.

*John 3:2–11. He was a challenging teacher.

Luke 20:9–18. Also *Matthew 13:53–58. He knew the sting of rejection.

*Mark 14:32–42. He suffered the deepest kind of sorrow.

*Mark 15:15–20. He was mocked and ridiculed.

Mark 15:21–34. He experienced the agony of feeling for-saken by His Father.

Week 14
"Follow Me"

When I was a young woman, just out of college in my first teaching job, I had a dream one night that was so vivid I can almost relive it now, even though many years have passed since then. I was a public school speech therapist, and I dearly loved my work. At last, after four years of preparation, I was finally doing the thing I'd been trained to do. In the dream, I was working with one of my favor-ite pupils, a darling little girl named Sally, who lisped. As you know, dreams sometimes have incongruous settings, and in this one, Sally and I were alone on a beach by the ocean, pouring sand out of cups as we made the *sssss* sound. I looked up and saw a man coming toward us. As he came closer, I saw that he was dressed in flowing white robes, and the robes seemed to be made of pure

light. I didn't ever see a close-up of the face, but I somehow knew it was Jesus. He didn't say a word—just made
a beckoning motion with His hand as He passed by us and
walked on. I knew He was asking me to follow Him, but
I didn't want to go. I was so happy to finally be doing what
I wanted to do. I didn't want to give it all up. Besides, I
couldn't leave Sally there alone, could I?

Jesus just kept on walking. I started after Him, plead-
ing with Him to excuse me from following just now, giving Him all the excuses I could think of. He just kept
going. I stood there, between Jesus and Sally, feeling
torn. Finally, I could see that Jesus would soon be out of
sight, and I ran to catch up with Him. When I came close
to Him, He opened His arms and I ran into His embrace.
Words are inadequate to describe the feeling of pure joy
I experienced at that moment in my dream. Then, very
gently, He picked me up and placed me back by Sally.
That's all there was to the dream, but its message was so
very clear that I've never forgotten it. Jesus calls me to
follow Him, to place Him first, before all earthly things.
But He never, never forces me. The choice is mine. If I
choose to follow Him, He is very likely to give me back all
I've given up—and more.

How gently, how persistently Jesus continues to call
His own to Him. His invitation is simple, with no promises of power, prestige, or possessions. But what a privi-
lege it is to receive a personal invitation from Jesus Himself.
When you were baptized, the words which He addressed
to His disciples became applicable to you: "As my Father
has sent me, even so send I you" (John 20:21). It's an
invitation to work with Him, walk with Him, live with
Him, enjoy victory with Him, celebrate life with Him.
Your call is a gift from God. "Ye have not chosen Me, but
I have chosen you" (John 15:16). His call places the desire
within your heart, that longing which helps you exclaim

with the man of the Gospel: "I will follow thee withersoever thou goest" (Matthew 8:19).

Then our Lord tells us that, as a condition of discipleship, we must give up being self-centered. Oh! How hard that is! In fact, it's impossible! That's why we need to surrender ourselves to Him *each day*, asking Him to send His Holy Spirit to help us die more to self today than we did yesterday. And always, he is there to help make the impossible possible.

This week, as you pray with Scriptures that show Jesus calling His followers, try to place yourself in the scenes, listen with your heart, and you will hear Him call you to follow Him.

Texts for Week 14

*John 1:35–51. The first disciples are called. (John the Baptist called the disciples to repentance. Jesus calls us to discipleship.) Enter the scene and feel *yourself* being called.

*Luke 5:1–11. Unworthiness is not a factor, not an obstacle.

Luke 9:23–26. The condition of following Jesus.

Luke 10:23–28. What is true discipleship?

Matthew 20:24–28. A disciple of Jesus must serve others.

*Matthew 19:16–30. Condition of discipleship: detachment from self and world, attachment to Jesus. Reward of renunciation.

*Luke 9:57–62. Jesus honestly warns about the hardships for those who follow His call. (What things do *you* put before Christ?)

Week 15
"I will teach you"

When my friend Carolmae ended our phone conversation

with " Have a blessed day," the words made me think.
What would a truly blessed day be like? Happy? Of course.
Peaceful? Yes. Love-filled? Definitely. But the dictionary
reminded me that it would be, above all, a *consecrated*
day. Then I thought of all the "blesseds" in Jesus' Sermon
on the Mount. I turned to Matthew 5 and as I read the
Beatitudes, it became clear that Jesus had given us a
pattern not only for a blessed day but for a truly blessed
life. This week, let's begin each day's prayer time by conse-
crating the day to our Lord. Then, instead of meditating
on several verses, let's spend our time contemplating just
one of the Beatitudes each day. Place yourself in the crowd
of followers who listened to Jesus as He taught on the
mountainside. See and hear with your faith, as Jesus speaks
to you. As you stand in the crowd, you will hear some say,
"This is a hard saying, who can hear it?" And you will see
them walk away. Let the strong desire well up in you that
you may be among those who remain.

First Day. Consider what it means to be poor in spirit.
Sometimes we strain so hard after spiritual experiences
that we miss the real thing. Be poor in spirit, empty before God, leaning on His love. Don't try to program your
prayer time. Ask God to empty your spirit to make room
for His Spirit.

Second Day. Bring all of your grief, all sense of loss,
both past and present, to Jesus. If this brings tears, that's
o.k. They are tears of release—a gift of God. Then allow
Him to enfold you in His fatherly arms.

Third Day. Offer everything you do, all day, to the Lord.
I'm sure the Lord is pleased with those who win many
souls for Him. But I believe He delights just as much in
those who lovingly perform *whatever* mission He has appointed for them, even if it seems relatively unimportant.
During the third day, offer everything you do, all day, to
Him. Stop for a moment before you begin each activity,

and dedicate it to Him; then do it quietly and humbly, without concern for personal gain or public recognition. You'll be surprised at the effect this will have on your day.

Fourth Day. Allow yourself to feel the deep hunger and thirst that God has placed within you. By the age of eighteen, Leo, a young friend of mine, had tried smoking, drinking, sex, and drugs and had finally decided that life was nothing but emptiness. Recently, he stood in my doorway with joy written all over his face. When I asked him why, he said, "Well, I discovered an amazing thing. God put that emptiness inside of me to draw me to Him. But I kept trying to fill it with temporary external things—until I realized that the only high that lasts is Jesus." Use the fourth day to let the love of Jesus pour in to fill up every inch of emptiness within you.

Fifth Day. Maybe, during your fifth day of praying with the Beatitudes, our Lord will show you a relationship that needs healing. Is there someone who has wronged you? You may be led to perform an act of mercy for that person. If so, try to follow through on it. God will heal you both.

Sixth Day. Try to keep your heart centered in Jesus all through this day. A friend told me that every time she feels worried, or tempted, or depressed, she closes her eyes and visualizes the face of Jesus until she can feel His love radiating within her. By human standards, this friend is rather plain looking, but she has a lovely golden glow about her that makes her seem truly beautiful. Maybe your sixth-day meditation will lead you to try my friend's way of keeping your heart centered in Jesus.

Seventh Day. What does being a peacemaker mean to you? I know I have to begin with myself. Today, I'll sit quietly in the presence of my Lord and let His peace soak into me. Then maybe I'll be able to radiate some of it outward into my family, my town, my country, God's world.

There are eight Beatitudes and only seven days in a week, so on the last day, after you've prayed about being a peacemaker, consider the fact that you may have to endure some persecution as you follow Jesus. He said that, if we put Him first, we might not always "fit in." Well, maybe it's not so bad to be a little different. The approval of others can't bring heavenly comfort or secure the Kingdom of Heaven. But trying to live the Beatitudes can. Jesus said so. Compared with the inner joy of living in Christ's presence, human disapproval fades into insignificance.

Texts for Week 15

Matthew 5:3. "Blessed are the poor in spirit."

Matthew 5:4. "Blessed are they that mourn."

Matthew 5:5. "Blessed are the meek."

Matthew 5:6. "Blessed are they which do hunger and thirst after righteousness."

Matthew 5:7. "Blessed are the merciful."

Matthew 5:8. "Blessed are the pure in heart."

Matthew 5:9–11. "Blessed are the peacemakers ... [and those] which are persecuted ... for my sake."

Week 16
"I will heal the sick"

Jesus came into the world not only to touch people's hearts and spirits but also their bodies. His concern was always for the whole person—body, soul, and spirit. There was only one thing He asked of those who came to Him for healing: "Do you believe I can do this?" I *do* believe that Jesus can heal, and I'm sure you believe it, too. But when I'm hurting or one of my loved ones is sick, it's sometimes kind of hard to believe that He *will* heal this ailment at this time. Once, when I was praying for God to heal my daughter of an excruciating headache, He showed me a way to strengthen my faith in His willingness to make her well. As I prayed, I heard her moaning in the other room, and suddenly I realized that I was praying for her wholeness while I mentally pictured her lying on the bed writhing in pain. At that point, my eyes fell on a photo of Karen and her boyfriend taken at the Senior Prom. In the picture, Karen was happy and healthy and pain-free. As I continued to pray, I began picturing her *that* way, instead of seeing her suffering. It wasn't long before the moans ceased and Karen fell into a peaceful sleep. When she woke up, the headache was gone. This is just one incident, but since that day I've tried to remember, whenever I pray for someone who is ill, to picture him or her in perfect health. It doesn't change God's willingness to heal the person (He always wants wholeness for His children), but it helps me to believe while praying.

Every week when our prayer group meets, we start by bringing our prayer list up to date, moving the names for which our prayers have been answered to the "Blessings Received" section. Recently, in going over our old lists, we were stunned and thrilled at the number of people our Lord had healed. With brimming hearts, we thanked God for the incredible way He had quietly moved through our lists, healing, comforting, blessing, providing, meeting all kinds of diverse needs. It's human nature to focus on those stubborn problems for which we can't see immediate results from our prayers and to fail to notice all those that have been answered. If you need a faith strengthener, try keeping a prayer list.

Or place yourself in the scene as Jesus heals a leper, a hemorrhaging woman, a deaf man, a blind man, and a little girl. After you've watched Him heal these people, mentally put yourself or the person you are praying for in the place of the one He healed and just let the Holy Spirit direct your visualization.

On the last day of the week, hear Jesus asking others to heal in His name. Know that His gifts of healing are still active in the world and that if you really believe that the risen Jesus dwells within you, you can lay hands (His hands) on the sick and be the vehicle through which His healing love flows into the sick person.

Texts for Week 16

*Mark 1:40–45. Cure of a leper.

*Luke 5:17–26. Cure of a man with palsy.

*Mark 5:25–34. Cure of a woman with a hemorrhage.

*Mark 7:31–37. Cure of a man who was deaf and mute.

*Mark 10:46–52. Cure of a blind man.

*Luke 7:1–10. Cure of the centurion's servant.

*Luke 9:1–6, Luke 10:1–12, and Mark 16:16–20 (all three for one meditation). Jesus asks others to heal in His Name.

Week 17
"This is the way to love"

I once had a neighbor who was a real troublemaker. She deliberately set friend against friend by making remarks such as, "You should *hear* what Mary said about the way you keep house!" Even when I'd try to be nice to her, I always seemed to end up on the defensive because of her needling. After one particularly trying incident, I said to a trusted advisor, "Jesus said I'm to love my neighbor, but how can you love someone who is so obnoxious?"

His answer was an eye-opener. "Jesus didn't say we have to love the *personality* of everyone we know. Just love the child of God within her."

That advice has helped me so many times, when I've been annoyed by someone or felt I just couldn't love a certain person. When I have those negative feelings, I admit to myself that I don't like the personality of that person, and then I try to send out love to the child of God within him or her. Sometimes as I do this, I glimpse a wounded, love-starved child in my adversary, whose silent screams cry, "Love me! Please! Please!" And my mothering heart can't help but respond.

There are times when even that doesn't work, though. Then I'm helped by something I read once about St. Thérèse of Lisieux. She prayed, "Lord, take my heart away and implant Your heart in me." Her idea was to open her heart so fully to God that He would fill her completely with His own love. She could then direct this Divine Love residing in her heart to all human beings. As soon as she prayed this way, her heart was possessed by a love so great and flaming that she was entirely transformed. All those who lived around her began to feel the radiation of this love.

I have prayed this prayer in many interpersonal situations, and it has never failed to have a positive effect on my feelings about the other individual.

Jesus said, "Love one another, as I have loved you" (John 15:12). Impossible! God loves me unconditionally. How could I, with all my human failings, love another as *God loves*? The good news is that, even though I am not capable of such love, His love flowing through me *is* able to accomplish the impossible!

You have probably known the joy of having God's love flow through you to others, in answer to prayer. But if you want to experience this in a more powerful way, choose a day, in advance, on which to make your offering of self. Prepare for it by prayer, Scriptural prayer, and meditation. Then ask God to take away your heart and implant His heart in you so that you may love Him and others with His own Love. Keep silence before Him until you feel His love welling up within you. Then give thanks and return to your daily tasks. During the day, whenever you have interaction with another person, remind yourself that it is God's heart that fills your chest. I'm not going to tell you what to expect. I'd rather have you discover it for yourself.

As you pray with this week's Scriptures, keep asking yourself what it would be like to love the way Jesus does.

Texts for Week 17

Luke 10:25–37. The first level of love: loving others as yourself.

Matthew 25:31–46. Second level of love: loving others as we love Jesus.

John 15:12–17. Third level of love: loving others as Jesus has loved you.

Luke 6:27–38. Fourth level of love: your love should be universal, including even your enemies.

John 17:20–26. Perfect love is union with God.

Romans 5:1–8. The Holy Spirit places the love of God in your heart.

John 13:31–35. The chief test of Christian discipleship.

Week 18
"I am"

When I was a teenager at church camp, the minister asked a question of our group. "What are the two most powerful words ever spoken?" Hands went up all over the tent.

"*Please* and *thank you*," said the girl with the delicate look.

"*Yes* and *no* are powerful words," said another girl.

"How about *Jesus* and *Christ*?" asked the boy next to me.

"*God* and *love* must be the answer," said another.

"All of those are powerful words," said the minister, "but even more powerful are the two words, I AM."

Then he proceeded to explain that *I AM* is the name of God the Creator. When God appeared to Moses in the burning bush and Moses asked His name, God replied, "I AM THAT I AM" (Exodus 3:14). And when the Jews asked Jesus how he could claim to know their forefather Abraham, He replied, "Before Abraham was, I am" (John 8:58).

The minister continued, "That's why we should be very conscious about how we use the words *I AM*. They are creative words, so that whatever follows them is likely to become true. Then he gave an example: "If I have an appointment for a job interview and I say to my wife, 'I am so nervous, I just know I am going to blow it,' then the chances are very good that I *will* blow the interview. If, on the other hand, I say, "I am poised and confident. I am the best candidate for the job," the likelihood of my getting the job is more than doubled."

Our mentor even went so far as to suggest that each of us choose one character trait we'd like to develop and then use "I am" as a form of prayer. Instead of praying, "Lord, help me to be more patient," we were to pray, "I am a very patient person. Every day I am becoming more patient, in the name of Jesus Christ." Since I was a rather shy young woman, my prayer was, "In the name of Jesus Christ, I am outgoing and friendly." By the end of our week at camp, I was truly amazed at the change that had begun to take place in me. I really was becoming a more outgoing person.

Here's something for you to think about. Since I AM is the creating name of God, what does that knowledge add to your interpretation of the third commandment: "Thou shalt not take the name of the Lord thy God in vain" (Exodus 20:7)? Could it mean that we are not to use the words, *I AM*, to express anything that is ungodly? What about Jesus' promise that whatever we ask "in His name" will be done? Could it be that every time we say "I am," we call forth that promise?

Regardless of how you answered the above questions, I think you'll agree that our teacher was very wise. It's true that what we say about ourselves, we begin to believe; and what we believe about ourselves, we become.

This week, let's look at some of the many ways *Jesus* used those all-powerful words. For example, instead of saying, "I *will be* resurrected," He said, "I am the resurrection and the Life." That isn't just a different way of speaking. It's a deeper truth. As you read this week's Scriptures, let each of our Lord's "I-am" statements rest on your heart for a while, without trying to figure out a meaning. It isn't a meaning you're seeking. It's a Being. If you are to discover fresh insights, He will present them to you as part of Himself.

Texts for Week 18

John 6:30–40.	"I am the bread of life."
Luke 22:19–27.	"I am among you as he that serveth."
John 8:12–23.	"I am the light of the world."
	"I am one that bear witness of myself."
	"I am from above."
John 10:1–10.	"I am the door."
John 10:11–18.	"I am the good shepherd."
John 14:9–21.	"I am in the Father."
John 15:1–11.	"I am the true vine."

If you have time, you may want to look up these passages, too:

Exodus 3:14

John 14:6
John 11:25
John 8:58
Matthew 11:29
Matthew 22:32
Matthew 27:43
Matthew 28:20

Week 19
"I offer you gentleness, compassion, forgiveness"

Recently, I received a letter which told about a wife-swapping situation the writer and her husband had been involved in for a couple of years. She had gone along with it because her husband had threatened to leave her if she didn't. She hated every minute of it, but most of all, she hated herself. "I stopped going to church," she wrote, "and I even stopped praying, because I hated myself so much and I knew Jesus must hate me, too. What right did I have to pray, when I was living such a sinful life?"

"Then my sister-in-law invited me to go to your retreat," the letter continued. "I agreed to go, even though I felt squeamish about the whole thing. When I saw 'Praying with Scripture' on the schedule sheet, I was sure I'd made a big mistake in coming. I can't stand people who go around quoting Scripture, and I never read the Bible," she wrote. "Then you told us to go to our rooms and spend a *whole hour* with a few lines of Scripture! I would have left at that point, except that I'd come in my sister-in-law's car and didn't have a way home. Well, I want to tell you that sometime during the second half of that hour, the man, Jesus stepped into that room. At first I was afraid, but He put His arms around me and I found out that He's the most gentle, compassionate, forgiving Person I've ever known."

The letter went on to tell that in the weeks that had passed since that time, she'd continued to pray with Scripture and that, with Jesus at her side, she'd told her husband she would never again participate in the immoral things they'd been doing. Much to her surprise, her husband seemed relieved! She said they're still having some marital problems, but that they have started praying together and she believes they're on the way to wholeness in their marriage.

A Scripture passage that I often use when teaching is John 8:2–11, about the adulterous woman Jesus had compassion for. When I used it that day I had no idea that someone there would have that problem. I just wanted people to experience Jesus' gentleness and compassion.

The Scriptures for last week told us what Jesus said about Himself. This week, we're going to watch Him in action, to discover, first-hand, His gentleness, compassion, kindness, forgiveness. This would be a good time to review the procedure for entering Scriptural scenes (See Week 12) and to use that way of praying to really experience Christ's presence. The lady who wrote to me had a problem that was similar to that of a character in the actual scene, but that isn't necessary for fully, joyfully entering into His presence in a Bible scene. Just *be there* and watch the scene happening. Then, whatever your problem is, step forward and ask Jesus for what you need—forgiveness, healing, love, security, reassurance, compassion—you know your own needs. Then allow Him to act according to the way you have just seen Him acting toward the people in the scene.

Texts for Week 19

*Luke 7:11–17. Jesus shows compassion for the widow of Nain.

*Mark 10:13–16. Jesus and the children. Gentleness and kindness.

*John 8:2–11. Gentleness, forgiveness to the adulterous woman. He accepts her the way she is at that very moment.

*Luke 18:35–43. Compassion and pity for the blind man.

*Mark 1:38–44. Jesus feels compassion for a leper.

*Matthew 15:32–39. He has compassion for the people and provides them with food. What are *your* needs?

*Luke 10:30–37. The good Samaritan. (When you enter this scene, first try being the injured man, and let Jesus be the Samaritan. Then, for a fresh and challenging experience, reverse these roles, as you minister to *Him*.)

Week 20
"I will help you fight temptation"

My prayer time last night centered on Matthew 21:12, which tells of Jesus throwing the merchants and money-changers out of the temple. I put myself in the scene and saw men selling all kinds of sacrificial animals during Passover time. I felt the stunned silence of the crowd as Jesus went striding into the temple, His jaw set and His eyes flashing. With an air of absolute authority, He overthrew the tables of the moneychangers and upset the chairs of those who were selling pigeons. Coins clattered to the floor. Birds' wings flapped madly. Merchants shouted in indignation. Then there was a shocked silence, and many stood with gaping mouths as Jesus said, "It is written, My house shall be called the house of prayer; but ye have made it a den of thieves."

My heart was pounding as I stood there in the scene, admiring my Lord. What power! What mastery! What courage! This is what I wrote in my journal: "What is it about this event that grips me, thrills me, makes me want to stand up and cheer? I know! It's that my Jesus, so gentle, so kind, is also a mighty and vigorous . . . *fighter*! As long as I stay close to Him, He will defend me, fight for me, purge my inner temple. If material things begin to clutter up my life, He will come striding in and overthrow the tables. If others try to rob or cheat me, He will knock them out of their chairs. If my carnal nature leads me into temptation, I can call His name and He will drive the animals out. Oh, what blessed security it is to have a gentle Friend who is also a fearless warrior in the battle against evil."

I felt (experienced deeply) the Christ within me doing battle with the evil within me. Oh, what a glorious, holy fight! This was a whole new kind of experience for me. A catharsis. An inner healing. A new wholeness. Normally, I'm a person who avoids conflict as much as possible, so I was really stunned by the inner violence I felt during this meditation, and even more surprised by my reaction of joy.

I concluded my journal notes with these words to my Friend Jesus, who fights for me: "I think you've given me something new and fresh and meaningful tonight, Lord— a new dimension to my relationship with you and with wholeness. The battle is long overdue. Go to it, Lord!"

All day today, I've felt lighter, lifted somehow, secure in the knowledge that my Lord is fighting for me. He fights for you, too. Let yourself experience this valiant Friend during your prayer time, and when temptation threatens, you'll know the inner certainty of the Victor's promise.

Texts for Week 20

*Matthew 21:12–13. He drives the moneychangers out.

*Matthew 4:1–12. Jesus understands how we feel when we are tempted because He, too, had to face the tempter.

Luke 22:28–32. Jesus prays for Peter to stay faithful.

(Peter fails only because he doesn't think he will be tempted.)

Romans 8:35–39. Nothing can separate us from the love of God.

I Corinthians 10:1–13. You will not be tempted beyond your ability to resist.

*Mark 10:17–27. Even when the temptation seems impossible, God can handle it.

James 4:7–10. When tempted, draw near to God and He will draw near to you.

Week 21
"I will set you free"

Anyone who has lived through adolescence and entered into adulthood knows that freedom is an elusive thing. The young man who thought that having a driver's license would set him free soon found out that he had to buy gas, and that made it necessary to surrender some free time to the task of earning money. The man who divorced his wife so he could be free to marry his secretary found himself no more free in his second marriage than he had been in the first. The young mother who thought she'd have lots of free time when her children started to school was surprised to find herself still spinning in circles after the last child entered kindergarten. So what goes wrong? Why is freedom so hard to come by? I believe it's not something that happens outside us. It's something that happens within us. Freedom is a state of mind. Once you are free in your mind and heart, you begin to be free in external things, as well.

I can hear you saying, "That's all very well, but how do I get free within?" I believe there is only one way, and that's through putting God first in every nook and cranny of your life. It's not allowing *anything* to become more important to you than God.

Now I don't mean to be standing up here on my soap box telling you what to do, because there are still only too many unfree areas in my own life. It's just that, through prayer and meditation, I've been learning to let go a little, learning to give things over to Christ, learning to get rid of (some of) my dependence on outer things. Believe me, I've still got a long way to go, but there's a visualization prayer that's helped me a lot, and I'd like to share it with you.

God gave this to me several years ago, when our oldest son, Paul, was in a coma in the hospital's intensive care unit, as a result of a car accident that had killed his girl friend. As I sat in the waiting room in the middle of the night, tired beyond belief but in too much emotional pain to sleep, I closed my eyes and murmured the only prayer I could manage, "God, help!"

Almost immediately I saw, in the blackness behind my eyelids, an opening in the dark. It looked like thousands of tiny pinpoints of light. It seemed to be above and slightly in front of me. Somehow I knew it was a representation of the Christ light. Right away, pictures started crowding my mind . . . Paul's cut and bleeding face, the face of his girlfriend's mother contorted with grief, Paul's totaled car, and many other horror pictures. Without words, God led me to pass each of those mental pictures up through that space of shimmering light. As each visualization passed through that filtering light, it was mercifully removed from my mind, passing completely out of my awareness. I don't know how long I continued in this unusual form of prayer, but it grew to include not only mental pictures, but words and whole thoughts. As each one came into my mind, I passed it through the shimmer of light and let it go. By the time I opened my eyes again, I felt new and free. That doesn't mean that I stopped caring or even that the emotional anguish was completely gone. It's just that God had separated me from it. I know, now, that the only thing I can never be separated from is Christ. All external things are as dust, and prayer can free me from attachment to them. In the final tally, nothing matters but God. This is the most liberating thing I have ever learned.

It has set me free . . .
>free to let God happen to me
>>free to be myself
>>free to be whole
>free to be a child of God, faith-filled, radiant
>>free to have an authentic faith
>free from dependence on the opinions of others
>>free from fear, loneliness, grief
>>>free from indecision
>>free from being manipulated
>free from being dominated by external events.

As you pray with this week's liberating Scriptures, let God speak through your inner light, that part of you that is eternally free.

Texts for Week 21

Isaiah 61:1–6. The Lord sent Isaiah to proclaim liberty to the captives.

Luke 4:16–21. Jesus has been sent to free those who are bruised.

John 8:31–36. If the Son makes you free, you are truly free. The truth makes you free.

Galatians 5:1, 13–18. Christ has made you free, but consider carefully how you use that freedom.

Jeremiah 31:10–14. The Lord frees you from your enemies.

*Acts 16:25–34. Paul and Silas are freed when they sing in their chains.

Psalm 51:1–12. Freedom from sin; being lifted up by the free Spirit.

Week 22
"I will help you overcome your anger"

I am writing this, sitting at the dining room table of our cabin in the Colorado Rockies. This little cottage came to me from my parents, who inherited it from my grandparents, so I've been vacationing here every summer since I was born. It has become a part of me. The cabin is not a fancy place, but it's situated in the midst of breath-taking beauty. I've spent many happy hours, sitting at this table, feeding my spirit on the view of the mountains as they rise steeply heavenward beyond our picture window.

My daughter Karen and I arrived here Tuesday night late and went right to bed. I woke Wednesday morning with a thrill of anticipation and did what I always do the first thing in the morning here. I walked into the dining room and looked out the window, hungry for spiritual nourishment. There's no way I can tell you how I felt when I saw a six-foot high, solid slab fence, completely blocking our view of the mountains. In fact, you can now see nothing but fence outside the picture window which had been our only view of the mountains. I'm sure our neighbors didn't realize what their fence would do to us, but I felt as if I'd been slapped in the face. My first thought was, "I can't believe this is happening!" Then, "How *could* they do this?" Hot tears stung my eyes as my hurt feelings gave way to anger. Suddenly, I was furious! I woke Karen and we fed each other's anger, with "Oh! What an eyesore!" and "Isn't that awful?" We grumbled around all morning until, by noon, a black cloud seemed to have settled over the cabin. Then it occurred to me that we had a choice. There was nothing we could do about the fence.

It was on their property and they had a right to their privacy. But it was up to us to decide whether or not we were going to let that fence ruin our vacation.

It isn't easy to give up anger. You can't just tell yourself to stop being mad and expect the emotion to go away. I know, because I've tried that and it doesn't work.

But there's a passage in Colossians that I've been praying with this week, and through it the Lord has given me a four-part plan for dealing with my negative emotions. I'm going to depart from my usual format and ask you to turn, with me, to Colossians 3:1–17, so I can share with you what He's given me. No doubt He'll have other things to say to you when *you* pray with it.

Verse 2—"Set your affection on things above, not on things on the earth." I can't think of a single instance in which my anger has been caused by anything *except* earthly things. How about you? So the first thing I needed to do Wednesday afternoon was to get quiet within and focus on God. I sat with my back to the dining room window and asked Jesus to take away my anger. Then I just sat there in the stillness, feeling myself surrounded by the white light of His presence. When thoughts about the fence came to mind, I just mentally fed them into His light and let them go. After five or ten minutes, the cloud began to lift—not completely, but some.

Verse 8—"But now ye also put off all these: anger, wrath, malice. . . ." At this point, I conversed with God, asking Him to show me how to "put off" my anger. The way that came to me was to write out my feelings, offer what I wrote to Him in prayer, and then burn the paper. I did this, not hiding or repressing any feelings, and I felt an enormous release.

Verse 13—". . . if any man have a quarrel against any: even as Christ forgave you, so also do ye." Having followed the preliminaries the Lord had given me, it was not so difficult, now, to forgive my fence-building neighbor.

Verse 15—"... and be ye thankful." As the final step in getting rid of my anger, God wanted me to find one thing in the situation that I could be thankful about. I had to think quite a while, and I even enlisted Karen's help. But then we thought of the fact that we could plant flowering vines on our side of the fence and create a beautiful display of color outside our picture window. I've always loved the purple clematis vines that grace my mother-in-law's fence but never before have I had a good place to plant them. This fence will make an ideal spot for the lovely vines. I'm still not happy about the fence, but I really am thankful that I now have a place for the vines. So I've been praying my thanks to my heavenly Father, and my anger has lost most of its steam.

There's another thing I can be thankful for about that fence. It caused me to ask Jesus to help me handle my anger, and He spoke to me so very personally, through His Word, and gave me a tool for living I'm sure I'll use again and again.

Texts for Week 22

Colossians 3:1–17. Listen for what Jesus wants to say to *you* in this passage.

Matthew 5:21–27. Get right with your brother before going to the altar.

Ephesians 4:26, 31, 32. "Be ye angry, and sin not: Let not the sun go down upon your wrath."

Romans 12:19–21: "If thine enemy hunger, feed him. . . . Be not overcome of evil, but overcome evil with good."

Ecclesiastes 7:7–10. About impatience and anger.

Nehemiah 9:16–20. Anger and God.

Romans 5:1–10. God does not condemn you because of your anger.

Week 23
"I invite you to share in My last meal with My disciples"

At a recent prayer retreat, I asked the participants to pray with Luke 22:15–20, in preparation for Holy Communion, which was to follow their Scriptural prayer time.

Don was a husky, talkative man, with a keen mind and a tendency to reduce everything to a logic-tight formula. He had caused some dissension in the group by arguing with what others said and making cynical comments about their beliefs. When we came together to share our experience in prayer before time for the Lord's Supper, Don was the first to speak.

"I couldn't seem to get past that word, *remembrance,* in verse 19," he said. "Jesus said I should receive the bread and wine *in remembrance* of Him. That word wouldn't let go of me, so I started to take it apart. The prefix, *re,* means *'to do again.'* So I guess what God wanted me to see was a whole new meaning for the word: RE-MEMBER — to become a member again."

"Now, I've been a member of the church all my life, so He couldn't have meant *that,*" Don continued. "Then the message became clear to me. I cannot come alone to His table. Jesus is only present for me in the bread and wine, to the extent that I come to communion *united with the rest of His body.* And I'm not to go to His table until this has been accomplished!"

Don looked at the floor, then at the ceiling, adjusted his shirt collar, and then said, "So what I'd like to say now is: I'm sorry I've been so bent on looking for differences in the way we worship. We are, after all, children of the same Father. For the rest of the weekend, I intend to try to focus on what we all have in common instead of exaggerating our differences." Don did a pretty good job of it, too.

Now it may seem that that was reading more into the word *remembrance* than was actually there. Nevertheless, God had something to say to Don, so He used that word to say it. It's just one more example of the fact that God can use any Scripture passage to say exactly what each person needs to hear at any given time.

This week's verses are very familiar ones, and this sometimes makes us think we already know what the message is. But if you'll suspend all previous interpretations and consider the overtones and ramifications of each word, you will hear what Jesus wants to say to you today.

Texts for Week 23
*Luke 22:17–20. The bread. The cup. The Body. The blood.
I Corinthians 10:15–17. One bread, one body.
Ephesians 2:8–15. The blood of Christ unites.
Hebrews 9:12–29. By His own blood He cleanses me.
John 6:47–58. "I am that bread of life."
I Corinthians 11:23–29. Examine yourself before you approach the Lord's Table.
*Luke 24:13–36 (especially verses 30, 31, and 35). "He was known of them in breaking of bread."

Week 24
"I give you My life"

This week, we're going to try to be united with Christ in His suffering and death, in order that we may be united with Him, more fully than ever before, in the glory of His resurrection. I ask you to become, in your imagination, the disciple Peter, and to live through the events of Holy Week as that disciple.

On the first day, walk with Jesus in His triumphal entry into Jerusalem. As Peter, experience the joy of the reflected glory of Christ, as people wave palms and shout "Hosanna!" Mull over in your mind your Master's words, "The Son of Man will be betrayed."

On the second day, watch as Jesus strides into the temple and chases away the moneychangers. (I know, you've already prayed with this episode, but do it now, as Peter. See it through his eyes and ask the Lord what he wants you to discover through this event.)

Then on day three, stand in the temple next to Jesus as the Sadducees and Pharisees fire cunning questions at your Lord. Hear Him answer with confidence and wisdom. Consider His answer to the question about the greatest commandment. Let His words rest on your heart until you hear what He wants to say to you through His answer.

Go to the home in Bethany for dinner. Sit next to the Lord and watch the woman come in, break the alabaster jar, and anoint Jesus. Pray that, like her, you may give your best without worrying about the cost, without caring what other people think.

The fifth day is a time of great agony for you, as Peter, for on this day you fall asleep when He has asked you to watch with Him, you slash off a man's ear in a moment of anger, and you flee when they arrest Jesus. Then you deny, three times, that you know the Lord. Let yourself feel all of Peter's shame. Then, as the cock crows, look up to the balcony and see Jesus standing there. Notice that, as the Master's gaze holds yours, there is not a trace of anger in his eyes—only sadness, forgiveness . . . love!

On Friday, hear the shouts of the mob: "Crucify Him!" Watch as the spikes are driven through His hands and feet. Hear His words from the cross, in the depths of your soul. Experience the desire to die with Him. Make a total offering of yourself to Jesus. Pray for the grace to carry your own crosses of rejection, hardship, and pain, move out of yourself . . . toward Him, toward others.

Live through Saturday as Peter—feeling the overwhelming disappointment that this Jesus you've believed in, the One you thought was the Christ, the Son of the Living God, is unbelievably, yet undeniably . . . dead. With Peter, cling to the faint hope that what He said about the third day might be true. Maybe your prayer today will be the one Peter heard the father of an epileptic child pray: "Lord, I believe. Help my unbelief."

Remember that we are praying with these crucifixion Scriptures not out of any morbid desire to experience pain for its own sake, but because, by suffering with Christ, we can more fully experience the joy of His resurrection. I suggest that you read through the Scripture passage for the day; then close your Bible and your eyes and live through what you have just read.

Texts for Week 24

Matthew 21:1–11. The triumphal entry into Jerusalem.

Mark 11:15–19. Casting out the moneychangers.

Matthew 22:23–40. Jesus is questioned by the Pharisees and Sadducees.

Mark 14:3–9. The woman anoints Jesus.

Luke 22:34, 39–51, 54–62. Peter fails the Lord, as you and I do.

Luke 23:27–46. Jesus is crucified.

Matthew 27:57–66. He is placed in the tomb. (You will have to use your imagination to know how Peter felt on Saturday, but if you have experienced the other events of this week through the disciple's eyes, you will know.)

Week 25
"I have conquered death. Come live with Me"

Many years ago during World War II, the minister of our church made a plea for families to invite soldiers for

Thanksgiving dinner, and my mother responded. The young man who came to our house was named George, and he was the most joyful person I had ever met. When Mother asked him if he was always so cheerful, George gave us a recipe for happiness that I've never forgotten, because it is absolutely unfailing. George said his father had given it to him. Here it is: *The way to make Romans 8:28 work is to practice Ephesians 5:20.* That translates: The way to make all things work together for good is by giving thanks always for all things.

Last week we suffered with Christ, through Peter's eyes. This week we're going to practice joy—the joy of Christ's resurrection. Again, try to *be there*, with Mary Magdalene, with Peter and John as they hurry to see the empty tomb. Feel their fear to risk believing, their suppressed hope. Let Thomas represent your own doubting nature, and let the risen Christ reassure you. Be one of the disciples on the road to Emmaus, allowing the realization to dawn on your heart that the One Who walks with you is your Lord and Saviour.

Try to begin every day this week with praise and thanksgiving. When you wake up, greet the Lord who is always with you. Remind yourself that you are a Christian, not because you subscribe to a certain creed or belong to a certain denomination. You are a Christian because the risen Christ now lives in you and goes with you wherever you are. Wherever your way to Emmaus takes you each day—to the office, to the grocery store, to a meeting, to your workplace, to a social gathering, know that the risen Lord is with you. Know that He is at your side. Try to keep an Easter joy in your heart all day, all week. If negative thoughts enter your mind, immediately ask Him to take them away. Then let them go! It *is* possible that all things can and will work together for your good, if you hold the joy of His presence in your consciousness, through praise and thanksgiving.

It will not be easy, and you will probably find yourself falling back into old ways of thinking. When this happens, do not be discouraged. Just begin again to sing your inner song of praise. This might well be the most valuable week of your life, because you may be "transformed by the renewing of your mind"!

Even though it may not be Easter time when you experience this, every day is the day of the risen Christ. If you find this to be a truly transforming experience for you (and it will be, if you allow it to be) you may decide to relive this prayer experience every year, during Holy Week and the week following Easter. It is something I return to, again and again, and it always seems to renew my spirit.

Texts for Week 25
*Matthew 28:1–10. The empty tomb. The angel's message.
*John 20:11–18. Jesus appears to Mary Magdalene.
*Luke 24:13–35. Christ appears to the two disciples on the road to Emmaus.
*Luke 24:36–43. Jesus invites the disciples to touch Him.
*John 20:19–29. Jesus appears to Thomas and removes his doubts.
*John 21:1–14. Jesus appears on the shore of Tiberias.
*John 21:15–23. Our Lord asks the assurance of Peter's love. He asks the same of you and me.

Week 26
"I am with you always. Look for Me in all things"

Taking our dog Oscar for his daily walks is a chore—something that has to be done to protect the carpets. For me, the walks are just a means to an end, but for Oscar they are the high points of the day—his chance to experience the changing seasons of the grass, to sniff the wind-drifted scent of wild plum blossoms, or to dance a silly little jig in the freshly fallen snow. One day last April, Oscar and I stopped by the stump of the cherry tree our son John had planted—the one we'd had to chop down after last fall's vicious wind storm had split it from crook to roots. As I stood there while Oscar sniffed the stump, I noticed an amazing thing. Pushing their way up out of that seemingly dead stump were two tiny green shoots—irrepressible evidence of the power of life. Suddenly I felt as if I stood on holy ground. The hushed and hovering presence of God seemed to fill the air. It was the kind of everyday miracle that's so very easy to miss, so easy to take for granted.

Some day during this week, after you've spent time with the day's Scripture, you may want to go for a praise walk. As you step outdoors, take a deep breath of fresh air, reminding yourself that, by the grace of God, it sustains your life.

As you walk, use your gift of vision to notice, enjoy, even caress the colors, shapes, textures, movements in everything around you. Give thanks to God for your eyes and for all the beauty He has created.

Stop for a few moments to really listen to all the sounds about you, savoring them and thanking God for your precious sense of hearing.

Then consciously experience the feeling of the sun and air on your skin. Pick up a few stones, some gravel or sand, and other objects of nature, enjoying your sense of touch, and give thanks.

Do the same for the senses of taste and smell, expressing your deep sense of appreciation to God for all of your senses.[1]

Let each day's Bible verses arouse in you an ever deeper sense of wonder for the miracle that God has created—your body, His temple.

Texts for Week 26

John 1:1–18. Christ is present in all the works of creation, including every human being (verse 9).

Colossians 1:9–23. Jesus is the Head of all creation.

Psalm 8. The wonder of God's creation.

Psalm 136. A litany of thanksgiving.

Colossians 3:1–4. Life-giving union with the glorified Christ.

Psalm 104. The majesty and greatness of God calls me to a life of praise and intimate union with Him.

Revelation 22:1–21. "The Spirit and the Bride say, Come."

NOTE

1. I am indebted to Sister Thelma Hall, R. C., for the idea on which I based the above Praise Walk.

Week 27

"I will give you peace"

My kids say I belong to the "peace-and-quiet" generation, and I guess they're right. The trouble is, I never seem to find enough of it. If the TV isn't blaring, the record player is, or else there's a wrestling match on the family-room floor, or the phone is ringing or the dogs are barking or there is a group of teen-agers dancing in the basement or eating pizza in the kitchen. I learned quite a few years ago that if I was going to have any peace at all, I'd have to find it in the inner kingdom.

That was when our Lord showed me a way to enter into His peace. I was praying with His words from John 14:27, "Peace I leave with you, my peace I give unto you," and I began to visualize a calm, crystal clear lake within me. It symbolized the soothing Christ presence, bathing me in His peace. I just held that picture in mind until I really felt His peace washing over me. Then, when I went back to my household duties amid the noise and confusion, I kept mentally coming back to that visualization. I was amazed to discover how much calmer I was, how much more in control I felt. I've been practicing this form of tuning in to His peace ever since, and it always seems to calm my inner seas. Oh, my nerves still get a bit jangled sometimes, but now I know that peace has more to do with what's going on inside me than with what's going on around me.

If you belong to the peace-and-quiet generation but live in a whirling world, you might try this way of building your own inner chapel. Jesus will do the rest. Or maybe a line from one of the other Scriptures for the week will become your peacemaker.

Texts for Week 27

Psalm 23. "He maketh me to lie down in green pastures."
John 14:27-31. He gives you His own peace.
Numbers 6:22-27. The peace blessing.
Psalm 85:7-13. Righteousness and peace belong together.
Isaiah 9:2-7. The Prince of Peace.
*Mark 4:35-39. Jesus calms the raging sea.
John 16:29-33. You can have peace, even in tribulation.

Week 28
"I am here to comfort you"

I met Wilma when I spoke at a United Methodist Women's conference in Wyoming. In the middle of my first talk, her eyes caught and held mine, and I could see that she was close to tears. At 7:00 the next morning, Wilma knocked on my door and asked me to pray with her. Her husband of many years had recently left her for another woman.

Wilma had prayed and prayed for him to return to her, but he was pressing for a divorce. They had tried counseling, but it hadn't helped. As we talked, I could see that Wilma had been very dependent on Stan. He was her whole life, and she felt lost and helpless without him. We prayed for a healing of hearts and for the comfort of the Holy Spirit for Wilma. She asked God to help her to keep from becoming bitter.

Not long after that, I received a letter from Wilma in which she wrote, "At 10:30 A.M. Wednesday, September 29, I was standing in my kitchen near the table. An indescribably beautiful new feeling completely flooded me. I knew it was the Holy Spirit that had come upon me and I had 'the peace that passeth all understanding. . . .' I know that whatever way my life goes, I can handle it now—because I'm not alone anymore. The Holy Spirit is with me. What a blessed comfort He is!"

I've heard from Wilma several times since then, and her marriage problem has not been resolved. But this woman, who was once so helpless and lost, is now sustained and strengthened by the Holy Spirit. She's going to be all right!

Catherine Marshall, in her book *The Helper*, points out the fact that the Holy Spirit is uniquely equipped to be a Comforter because He acts and forms relationships that are only possible with a Person. It's wonderfully comforting to me to know that, when I feel rejected by others, when I am insecure and fearful, when all human helpers have left, I have an ever-present Comforter who will never leave me nor forsake me.

This week, let's try to become better acquainted with this marvelous Comforter.

Texts for Week 28
John 14:16–18. The Comforter shall be in you.

Acts 2:1–18. The Pentecost miracle is available to you today.

John 14:23–27. The Holy Spirit is your best teacher.

John 16:7–14. The Holy Spirit glorifies Jesus.

Ezekiel 36:25–28. "I will put my spirit within you."

Luke 11:5–13. Ask your heavenly Father for the Holy Spirit, and you will receive Him.

Romans 8:18–26. The Holy Spirit will help you in your weakness.

Week 29
"I will pray in you"

Occasionally someone will ask me, "How can you be sure the message is from God and not from Satan?" This need not be a big problem for the child of God who is protected by the Holy Spirit.

When you sit down with your Bible, before you begin to read or pray, or even to mark the passage, commend your heart, mind, soul, spirit, and every part of your being, *including your subconscious mind*, to the Holy Spirit. Then, call on the Spirit to guide and direct every moment of your prayer time and ask Him to pray within you. He will do it! (Romans 8:26)

There are many times when I'm not really sure what God's will is in a certain situation. For instance, I am frequently asked to pray for people who are considered terminally ill. I used to hesitate because, if I prayed for healing and it didn't happen, I was afraid the family might lose faith. On the other hand, God does perform miracles every day. Now, before I pray for a critically ill person, I take time, privately, to go to God and ask His will. Then I invite the Holy Spirit to pray in and through me. I've found that, as I pray, He supplies me with the right words. I always pray that God will relieve the patient's suffering; sometimes He leads me to pray that the person will have the grace and courage to bear his illness to the glory of God; sometimes I'm led to pray that some permanent good will result from this seeming evil, and sometimes the Holy Spirit gives me the nudge to pray for complete healing. I've learned that I can trust Him to pray God's will through me, but I *must* invite Him to do so.

Another time when I specifically call on the Holy Spirit is when I have a tough decision to make. He helps me to hear God's guidance. Before I begin my Scriptural Prayer, I ask the Holy Spirit to open my ears to God's message for me in regard to the problem. It still amazes me that He can and *does* use whatever the day's Scripture is to speak to me about that very specific situation.

Recently, I had to decide whether or not to attend a two-week training course in Spiritual Direction. I had been wanting to do this for a couple of years, but I always backed down at the last minute because I felt I shouldn't be away from my family for that long. This year, though, I felt a greater pull toward the course because I knew it would help me with a book I'm planning to write, after I finish this one. Still, I felt slightly guilty about being away from my husband and 15-year-old son.

So I asked the Holy Spirit to guide me in my Scriptural Prayer toward the right decision. The Scripture for the day, in the devotional booklet I use, was Matthew 6:24–34. I got all the way down to verses 33 and 34: "But seek ye first the kingdom of God, and his righteousness; and all these things shall be added unto you. Take therefore no thought for the morrow: for the morrow shall take thought for the things of itself."

For most people most of the time, this passage is blessed reassurance that their material needs will be provided. But this day, God said to me that I should put Him first and not worry about tomorrow—that He would take care of my family. I knew that was God's intention because the Holy Spirit completely lifted the burden of indecision from me in that moment, and I was filled with joy and certainty. Still, I think it's important to wait for confirmation—evidence that supports the decision. I didn't have to wait long. John was invited to spend a few weeks with our oldest son and his family to help out with the children. He was delighted and could hardly wait to go. And when I told my husband I really felt I should take the course, he agreed.

Texts for Week 29

John 4:21–24. God is Spirit.

John 6:53–63. Jesus' words are Spirit.

Romans 8:1–17. The Spirit dwells in you.

Romans 8:22–28. When you don't know what to pray for, the Spirit will intercede for you.

Romans 15:15–19. You are sanctified by the Holy Spirit.

I Corinthians 2:9–16. The Holy Spirit teaches you about spiritual things.

II Corinthians 3:15–18. "Where the Spirit of the Lord is, there is liberty."

Week 30
"I am the Living Water"

When I was a young woman, I knelt by the altar in a little brown church in McCook, Nebraska, and gave my life to Jesus. In return, He placed a spring of living water within me, but it wasn't until I began praying with the Bible that I learned to really drink from that well.

In John 7:38 and 39, Jesus tells us that the living water He offers us is the Holy Spirit. He also tells us where this spring is located: "He who believes in me, . . . Out of his *heart* shall flow rivers of living water" (RSV. *Italics added*).

This week, let's try to really experience the flow of the living water within us. This will demonstrate another approach to praying with your Bible. I'd like to invite you to join with me in a guided meditation based on Biblical promises about the action of the living water—the Comforter—the Holy Spirit.

A guided meditation is a visualization, but it's not just random daydreaming. It's visualization with purpose and direction. At first, this type of prayer may seem like mere fantasy to you, but if you'll open yourself to it, you'll soon become aware of a deep inner sense of validity in the experience.

LIVING WATER MEDITATION

After you have read and prayed with the day's Scripture, just close your eyes, relax, and allow the living water to cleanse you, comfort you, heal you. The first few times you use this method, read my text below until you come to a + sign; then close your eyes and experience that part of the visualization before continuing. After you've done this several times, you will be able to do it without referring to the book. You may want to return to the living water meditation again and again. It doesn't have to be limited to just this week.

Begin by directing your attention to a spot right in the center of your chest, at about the place where your ribs begin to separate. Take three long, slow, deep breaths, and just relax.

Now visualize a tiny trickle of water, beginning to bubble up from that spring that our Lord has placed within you.+

As the water flows into every part of your being now,

let go of all striving, all struggle, all tension. You are safe, cared for, protected, loved. Just let go. It's all right. Trust Him. If there's anything you're feeling guilty about, just ask His forgiveness now, and let His cleansing waters flow through you, washing away any ugly stains, cleansing you from all sin. Feel yourself being deeply cleansed in body, soul, and spirit.+

Have you been burdened by mistakes you've made in the past? Maybe you've made some mistakes in raising your children, or in your home life or your career or social life. Maybe you've done something that's embarrassed you that you haven't been able to let go of. Realize that God can take any mistake and turn it to good. Psalm 138:8 says, "The Lord will perfect that which concerneth me." He can and He will, so just feed all of those mistakes into the stream of living water and let them go. Give them to the Holy Spirit. He will overturn them.+

Now, let those living waters flow into your heart, healing any old hurts, any feelings of rejection, any buried resentments. Just let them all wash away in the love of God. If there's any grief or sense of loss, feed it into the stream, allowing the Holy Spirit to release you from all of that old pain that has accumulated within you.+ (If this brings tears, they are tears of release—a gift from God.)

Now that one big problem, that nagging worry that just won't go away—and we all have at least one of those. Pause a minute to again visualize that spring of water within you, near your heart. Let it become a fountain, spurting up, shooting up through the top of your head, rising up to the Father. Feel its power. Place that big problem or worry into the water and let it rise up to Him. Give it up. Let it go, and now let it pass completely out of your awareness, knowing that "the Lord will perfect that which concerneth me."+

If you are in any kind of physical pain, if you have any physical problem that needs healing, let those living waters flow over the area that hurts, or the area that's diseased or ailing. Just let the water stroke away the pain— soothing, comforting, restoring, healing. As the living water spreads throughout your body, allow it to renew, revitalize, restore each cell, healing, perfecting, through the love of Jesus Christ.+

Give thanks in the deep, deep part of your heart, carrying away with you that Spring that will always be with you, and turning to it often for refreshment and renewal and cleansing.

Texts for Week 30

Jeremiah 17:12–14. When we lose our deep-in awareness of the presence of the Spirit, we become spiritually dehydrated.

Zechariah 14:8–11. When our Lord enters the gates of our city within, He brings refreshment and renewal.

*John 4:5–14. The living water is inexhaustible.

John 7:38–39. His love fills us to overflowing

Romans 8:9–17. The Spirit of God dwells within us.

Revelation 7:13–17. It is Christ who leads us to the Holy Spirit.

Isaiah 58:8–11. The Holy Spirit, planted within us, causes us to grow in grace.

PART IV

Where Do We Go From Here?

"Be thou faithful unto death, and I will give thee a crown of life"

Revelation 2:10

IN Part I of this book, I told you that after you had been praying with the Bible for a while, you would no longer need the "wee bit pattern." After the first couple of weeks, you were no doubt able to have your Scriptural prayer time without referring to the procedural instructions. I hope, though, that you have continued to follow the themes for the thirty weeks.

By your faithfulness, and with the help of God, you have now prayed your way through two hundred and ten of the Bible's most meaningful passages. If you have stayed with it, you are without a doubt much, much richer in spirit than you have ever been before, and your relationship with our Lord has grown in intimacy and depth.

SOME PRACTICAL SUGGESTIONS

Where will you find themes and Scriptures for your future prayer times? There are several possibilities.

Maybe you'll want to do what I do. Using a daily devotional booklet, I look up the Bible passages given for each day and pray with those Scriptures. Most denominations publish their own daily devotional material, and all of these use Scripture as the basis for their meditations. Or you might use your church's daily lectionary in the same way. One nice thing about using a lectionary is that many of the denominations use the same Bible passages for each day of the church year, so you will be joining with other Christians as you pray with these Scriptures. If you aren't sure whether or not your church has a lectionary, check with your pastor.

If you ask at your local Christian book store, they will be able to supply you with a lectionary or devotional volume that can serve as a guide for your daily time in praying with God's Word.

As a variation on the above, I sometimes choose one of the books of the Bible and read through it, a few verses each day, stopping where the Lord directs.

Or, you could use the Table of Contents of this book to put you in touch with Scriptures that will speak to your various needs. Even though you have already prayed with these Scriptures, your meditations with them will be different every time you pray. Jesus will stop you at different places this time than He did before, and what He chooses to say to you today will be different from what He said to you the last time.

I pray that your experience with Scriptural prayer has been so rewarding that you will want to continue it for the rest of your life.

APPENDIX

Some Scripture Quotations for Walking Prayer

Here are some one-liners to use if . . .

a. *You have many problems:* "God is our refuge and strength, a very present help in trouble." Psalm 46:1

b. *You are doubting, perplexed:* "Teach me what I do not see." Job 34:32 (RSV)

c. *You are feeling guilty:* "Create in me a clean heart, O God." Psalm 51:10

d. *You're nervous about something:* "In quietness and in confidence shall be your strength." Isaiah 30:15

e. *You are lonely:* "Lo, I am with you alway, even unto the end of the world." Matthew 28:20

f. *You have work to do:* I will "Serve the Lord with gladness." Psalm 100:2

g. *You don't want to be where you are:* "Surely the Lord is in this place; and I knew it not." Genesis 28:16

h. *You face a busy day:* "Consecrate yourselves today to the Lord." Exodus 32:29

i. *You are traveling:* "The Lord your God is with you, wherever you go." Joshua 1:9 (RSV)

j. *You have heard some gossip:* "Set a watch, O Lord, before my mouth." Psalm 141:3

k. *You are depressed:* "When I sit in darkness, the Lord shall be a light unto me." Micah 7:8

l. *You are afraid to face someone:* "Perfect love casteth out fear." I John 4:18

m. *There is discord in your home:* "Peace be to this house." Luke 10:5

n. *You are in love:* "Many waters cannot quench love, neither can the floods drown it." Song of Solomon 8:7

o. *You feel weak:* "Be strong in the Lord, and in the power of his might." Ephesians 6:10

p. *You have a hard decision to make:* "Trust in the Lord . . . he shall direct thy paths." Proverbs 3:5-6

q. *You are impatient:* I will "rest in the Lord, and wait patiently . . ." Psalm 37:7

r. *Someone has wronged you:* I will "overcome evil with good." Romans 12:21

s. *You are very tired:* "Cast thy burden upon the Lord, and he shall sustain thee." Psalm 55:22

t. *You are tempted:* "He will not let you be tempted beyond your strength." I Corinthians 10:13 (RSV)

u. *You are in pain:* "The eternal God is thy refuge, and underneath are the everlasting arms." Deuteronomy 33:27

v. *You are sick:* "For when I am weak, then am I strong." II Corinthians 12:10

w. *You are afraid:* "What time I am afraid, I will trust in thee." Psalm 56:3

x. *You are unable to sleep:* "He giveth his beloved sleep." Psalm 127:2

y. *You are grieving:* "As one whom his mother comforteth, so will I comfort you." Isaiah 66:13

z. *You have financial worries:* "My God shall supply all your need." Philippians 4:19

No problems or worries? "Bless the Lord, O my soul: and all that is within me, bless his holy name!" Psalm 103:1 (*)

---

*Some of the above quotations were selected by Avery Brooke in *Hidden in Plain Sight: The Practice of Christian Meditation* (New York, N.Y.: Seabury Press, 1978).